Footprints of Fire
(The Black Eagle Book of Modern Odia Poetry)

Footprints of Fire
(The Black Eagle Book of Modern Odia Poetry)

Translated and Edited by
Bhagaban Jayasingh

BLACK EAGLE BOOKS
2019

BLACK EAGLE BOOKS
7464 Wisdom Lane
Dublin, OH 43016
E-mail: info@blackeaglebooks.org
Website: www.blackeaglebooks.org

First International Edition published by
BLACK EAGLE BOOKS, 2019

Footprints of Fire
(The Black Eagle Book of Modern Odia Poetry)
Translated and Edited by **Bhagaban Jayasingh**

Copyright © **Bhagaban Jayasingh**
Copyright of original poems are with individual poets

All rights reserved. No part of this publication may be reproduced, stored in a retrieval system, or transmitted, in any form or by any means, electronic, mechanical, photocopying, recording or otherwise without the prior permission of the publisher.

Cover & Interior Design: Ezy's Publication

ISBN- 978-1-64560-030-5 (Paperback)
Library of Congress Control Number: 2019953800

Printed in United States of America

INTRODUCTION

In a Sanskrit verse "Bharat Geetika," Radhanath Ray, the chief exponent of the late 19th-century Romantic poetry, said of Odisha as the "dala" (petal) of the "pankaj" (lotus) called India. The 11th-century religious text *Kapil Samhita* describes the state as the best in India, stating that there is no land as beautiful and spectacular as Odisha, variously called Utkal, Kalinga and also Orissa in the recent past. Odisha is the new official name of the state and its language, earlier called Oriya, has come to be known as Odia. A member of the Indo-European family of languages, this language, which is about 1000 years old, is spoken by 36.6 million people in Odisha and elsewhere. The state of Odisha was founded on the linguistic basis on April 1, 1936, and the change of name occurred only after a constitutional amendment happened in November 2011.

Odisha's contact with the West dates back to the early sixteenth century when the state was going through very bad times. It was getting increasingly difficult on the part of the Gajapati king of Puri to rule over such a vast territory, stretching from Ganga in the north to Godavari in the south. A century later the Portuguese traders landed in Odisha to spread the network of their trade and commerce. Then the Dutch followed in the footsteps of the Portuguese to settle in Odisha as traders.

But the real British contact, which was very significant for Odisha, began when the British merchants got permission to establish their factories in the state, beginning in 1633. Later the East India Company under Lord Clive got the Dewani authority of "Bihar, Bengal and Orissa" which had already come under one administrative unit during the Moghul rule. The Britishers who were earlier happy about their commercial interest slowly and steadily shifted their activities to political field. A conspicuous absence of any consistent resistance and for the lack of any credible leadership paved the way for the invading British force to occupy Odisha, the last of the Indian states to fall under British rule in 1803.

The process of modernization kicked off only after the people of Odisha came in contact with the Western ideas and values through the Britishers. The process was accelerated with the establishment of new English schools and printing press which brought about a steady transition from the *tal*-leaf manuscripts to print culture. The Western contact facilitated a steady transformation in the attitude and the outlook of the people and encouraged the writers to reflect the impact in their creative endeavors. The writers like Fakir Mohan Senapati, Radhanath Ray, and Madhusudan Rao planted the seeds of new literature around the 1860s. They are regarded as the greatest pioneers of modern Odia literature, and each of them ushered in a new trend in one's own field: Fakir Mahan in prose fiction, Radhanath in romantic poetry and Madhusudan in devotional lyrics of high intensity. They pioneered a movement to free the conventional forms of expression such as *chhand, chautisha,* and *champu*, besides some folk forms like *pala, dasakathia,* and *harikatha*. The Western literary forms liberated the pioneers of poetry from the shackles of these hackneyed literary forms and secured them easy access to the Western sonnet, ballad, ode, elegy, and lyrics. Exposure to these European forms brought about a revolutionary transformation in expressing a wide range of feelings and thoughts.

By the mid-fifties, after India got her freedom from the British occupation, the Odia writers had already obtained a fair measure of access to the Euro-American poetic traditions. They began to read the major twentieth-century English language poets like Yeats, Frost, Ezra Pound, TS Eliot, and many others. They also enjoyed poetical works of major French poets like Baudelaire, Mallarmé, Arthur Rimbaud and Jules Laforgue. The advent of new city culture, mass communication, information technology like radio, cinema widened their area of interest in Western modernism. The Odia poets grabbed every opportunity to cross their native boundaries in their attempt to completely overturn the traditional modes of expression. Driven by their passion to do so something new and different, they made every attempt to practice Ezra Pound's slogan "Make It New."

Sachidanda Rautray, popularly known as Sachi Rautray, emerged as the central figure of the post-independence Odia poetry. As the 'founding father' of the modernist movement of Odia poetry, he is most appropriately described as "Matir Drona," an epithet Rajendra Kishore Panda, a very significant Odia poet of the 70's, coined to mark his overwhelming impact on the generations of young poets who followed him to write new poetry. With the publication of *Pandulipi* (1947) and *Kabita 1962* (1962), Sachidananda turned to metaphysical mode of writing, though in the early phase of writing he wrote in revolutionary vein. He began to acquire "a mind and sensibility which could devour any kind of experience" —

a quality of the metaphysical poetry that Eliot praised so eloquently. Odia poetry for the first time became difficult, complex, sophisticated and technique-oriented. Sachidanand has been greatly admired for being the harbinger of a new poetic movement which was going to stay for a long time. He was the first poet who emphasized the relation of poetry to common speech. He made a fervent plea for the use of free verse, which, according to Sachidanand was "an unconventional language" to best express man's "love and tears, griefs and joys."

I have included in this anthology an unconventional poem named "Pratima Nayak," a poem that had shaped the contemporary poets' attitude to women. Pratima Nayak was no paragon of beauty, excelling in all womanly virtues, which the traditional poets celebrated in their verse. On the contrary, she was "sick from diseases," her face looked ugly, scared by pimples when her "dull" cheeks reflected "futility/ of unpretentious scars." Interestingly, Pratima wore no saree, the traditional attire of a woman of grace and beauty but was "wrapped in/ khaki."

Guruprasad Mohanty had also painted the social fabric of his time with some "new" women at the center of his creation. In some of his poems he depicted women who cannot think of a meaningful and lasting relationship with men. These men are depicted as perfidious seducers who chase women surreptitiously. Needless to say that Guruprasad's reputation lies not merely for creating "new" women but in the successful use of myth in poetry. "Kalapurusha," a long poem of more than 400 lines, established him as an outstanding poet of new taste and sensibility. This poem has been praised for being a monumental work in which Guruprasad made persistent efforts to grasp the international dimension of experience.

The poem was based on the contemporary experience of, what Eliot called in the European context, the "futility, and anarchy," which had "set in contemporary culture and civilization." In the poem "The Doves of My Eyes," he dwelt upon "sickness and death" suggested through a welter of images like the "rumpled" clouds, "desolate" moon and the leaves falling in *chaitra*.

Ramakanta Rath came into eminence in the mid-sixties when Sachidanand was at the peak of his literary career and Guruprasad had almost ceased to write. Though he incorporated into his work some traits of their poetic themes and techniques, Ramakanta started basically as a die-hard experimentalist. Ramakant's experiments with theme and technique of writing went well with the readers; they found in his work a new expression of reality. The reality was one of boredom and despair when man burns like a "lanthan" (lantern), and like the lantern he finds his existence "aflame." The poet described him burning in "a medium *dhoti*," and "a half-shirt trimly ironed" — a typical situation in the poetry of his early poetic career. As he moved forward in his poetic journey his poetry turned out to be ascetic in character. One cannot afford to miss "the low voice" of the poet on "deep matters" of life's experience. His journey from "the noiseless deep forest" assumed significance as he began to speak like a "mendicant."

As a mendicant-poet Ramakanta wrote *Sri Radha*, which contains sixty-one poems in all. The poet handled Krishna motif in this long poem. Writing on an over-emphasized theme was no less daunting. In the past, the poets wrote on the "mirror image" of Radha with a view to glorifying a love that was non-existent and even unrequitable. But Ramakanta explored the fresh ground by emphasizing the importance of passion and intimacy, the agonizing moments of loneliness and suffering in relationships, which are central to the experience of love. Mark the opening lines of the poem included in this anthology:

> When you touched me for the first time
> all the emptiness within me
> reverberated with sound
> It seemed you called me from all directions
> for what I could have become
> from their longing.

Sitakant Mahapatra, one of the best poets of post-independence India, is not a poet of love in the strict sense of the term. But in "Love of a Dhangra," the tribal youth, as he professes his love for the girl of his community, has demonstrated all the overwhelming passions of love. He is ready even to "gouge out" the pair of his eyes and offer them like "lotus flowers" for a mere "chunk of place/ in the nest" of her body:

> I asked to give me a touch, your life
> for my fluttering soul
> I asked you for a chunk of place
> in the nest of your body
> You said, I could see in the mirror of your
>   eyes
> everything looks lucent
> Not now, not now.
> ... ...
> I said, take, and now give me a touch,
> Love and darkness
> Give me some balm for my ulcerated soul.

The poem is born out of his anthropological interest in the oral traditions of tribal poetry. As an Indian Administrative Service officer, Sitakant had the experience of working in the tribal areas of the state. He had made an extensive scholarly study of tribal societies, their art, and culture. Emphasizing the relevance of tribal poetry to the modern world he said, "I feel primitive poetry has relevance today: not merely as "poetry" as CM Bowra had so ably analyzed, but as adding a significant dimension of meaning and purpose to the business of living and dying. Most often the city in his poetry moves to the forest to meet the "savage"- a term Eliot found to be extremely popular in the anthropology of the day. We also find the savage in his poetry undertaking a journey to the city to become a part of the city culture.

Rajendra Kishore Panda, Haraprasad Das, and Soubhagya Kumar Misra are the most significant poets of the '70s, who have made significant contributions to the enrichment of the poetry of this period. Of the three, Haraprasad is a restlessly experimental poet, trying every form of poetry from lyrics to odes, from ghazals to poetry in free verse. What attracts most about his poetry is the way he dwells upon everydayness of experience as documented in the poem "Infinity." He is so engrossed with day-to-day experience that he finds no time even to think about death. It is because he has "wrapped up a deal" with the Infinite:

> I cannot say it now
> Even if I had time
> I could never tell it to the neighbor
> who has trespassed into my house,
> I have already wrapped up
> a deal with the Infinite.

Rajendra Kishore Panda is also a powerful poet of this period with a large following.

Many of his poems explore the theme of *carpe diem*

(seize the day) and investigate the role of man in the universe. There is a sign of great courage and strength in his work, particularly when the poet uses words for right effects. He has often demonstrated his poetic ability to make his concerns public on social issues. He never leaves an opportunity to scoff at the system which is detrimental to man's interest. One can mark the tone of his poetic lines when he derided the state of emergency which was clamped down in 1975. His words "Anam Das, Adham Das/ Fire your first bullet at me" drips with sarcasm.

Soubhagya Kumar Misra is a different kind of poet; right from the publication of *Nai Panhara* (Swimming in the River), he articulated a voice that is unflinchingly and even ruthlessly authentic. Though Soubhagya's highly individualized response to life is often marked by deliberate word-play for effect for its own sake and ambiguities, they also signal his power and potentiality as a poet of some substance. The story of a monkey and the crocodile is dug out of the Jataka tales. Native to India these tales are based on the previous births of Gautama Buddha in both human and animal form. Though the poem appears to be simple, as simple as any tale, the elusive nature of its language has made it somewhat difficult. Soubhagya usually adopts a style that is at once quotidian and elitist; the elusive, and at times, the 'hermetic' manner of expression has often made him a difficult poet.

The poetry in the hands of poets from Binod Nayak, Uma Shankar Panda, Bibhudatta Mishra to Banshidhar Sarangi, Saroj Ranjan Mohanty, Devdas Chhotray and Phani Mohanty became romantic, and their poetry, as different from the highly complex and difficult writings of their times, got them closer to reader's hearts. Reading these poets became akin to walking through a gallery of love and tears, grief and solitude, loss and transcendence. They are all poets of exquisite elegance and composure. Binod and Uma Shankar, who mostly write on love and romance, try to strike a balance between the body and the mind, the physical and the spiritual. But the ambiguous fusion of the animal and the religious marks the poetry of Bibhudatta, and Devdas in particular who makes the fusion possible when he discovers honeybees all over the body of a little girl in frock ("Baby, look there are honeybees all over your frock.") Saroj and Phani Mohanty have never put sexuality at the center of their creation; they have never indulged in the vulgar display of love as the manifestation of the base human instinct. Phani in *Priyatama* (The Ladylove) and Saroj in *Kagaj Dangar Shoka* (The Sorrow of a Paper boat) celebrate love as something pure and godly, and their poetry evokes a feeling of purity and religious asceticism. As Phani believes

> The story of million loves
> never ends
> like the poet's story
> that transcends time and space
> on every lip.

Prasanna Kumar Mishra and Sourindra Barik are also the poets of love and romance. Most often their poetry is seen as a contrast between the past glory and the present squalor, the squalor represented by Prasanna's protagonist Sanatan on a truck or the cyclist of Sourindra's cycle poems. They ruminate over the aesthetic charm and elegance of the past to get rid of the shoddy and shameful way they live their lives now. The poetry written by Harihar Mishra, Praharaj Satyanarayan Nand and Pramod Kumar Mohanty is not romantic; there is an undercurrent of mystical thoughts that determines the tone and tenor of their creation. Banshidhar Sarangi is basically a poet of nature, and unlike the early Romantics who wanted to spiritualize nature at every opportunity, he looked at nature with the eye of the aesthete and turned natural object into poetic images. The poetry of Harihar who writes on the principle of poetic asceticism revolves around the Jagannath temple and its culture of universal brotherhood. His obsession with the past is always garbed in metaphysical abstractions, and this is the reason as to why his poetry appears to be difficult and complex to a casual reader.

The period between 1960 and 1970 marks the rise of a good number of women poets like Brahmotri Mohanty and Prativa Satapathy. The essential subject matters Brahmotri's poetry is built upon personal loss, private love, sex, memory and nostalgia. Born into a very orthodox Hindu family, she could not resist expressing some unorthodox inner feelings, like the ones she did in the poems like "After My Legs Slipped" and "The Strange Desires." The poem "Strange Desires" presents, though not ruefully, the lust of flesh through an intricate web of emotions. Bored with a conventional and 'sterile' type of love or sex, she is driven by a 'strange,' fleshly desire she states:

> In moments of an intense desire
> I wish: You should fling me into the air
>   like a ball
> and by stretching your arms
> clasp me when squealing in excitement
> I begin to fall on the ground.
>
> Or, on the bank of a river,
> pretending to show me its blue water
> you could push me into its water
> and then pluck me from there

when in shock and awe with my eyes
> closed

I could hold you tight

In the dense cloudless autumn.

The whole poem seems to subscribe to the Freudian theory of art as a sublimation of repressed sexual energy.

Like Brahmotri, Prativa Satapathy is also a poet of spectacular gifts, but when Brahmotri creates a world of genuinely revelatory and confessional poetry, Prativa resorts to reason and restraint to create a world of her own. Unlike Brahmotri who never regrets 'being a woman,' Prativa expresses her helplessness as a woman and wails over her fate, saying she is always tortured by "Man/ whether he is god or human or devil/ husband, lover or robber." There are certain qualities in her poetry which may be called glitteringly feminine: love, generosity, compassion, tenderness and humility. Her poem "My Youngest Son" is based on an overwhelming sense of regret and loss: regret unfulfilled joy which reminds one of Charles Lamb's "Dream Children." A reverie as it is called, it has all the pain of lost hope and unfulfilled desire as well. She imagines the child descending down her womb when "the brook of my breasts/ would have gone dry/ my lap would have looked empty/ like a crumpled loaf of bread." As the poem concludes, her lost motherhood comes as a terrifying experience:

You would come

... ...

as I would hasten to embrace you

you a fragile bridge would have collapsed

before your eyes.

Mamata Dash, Binapani Panda and Swapna Mishra are deservedly some of the talented poets writing in Odisha now. They are endlessly adroit in creating poems as a network of feminine emotions and thoughts. Aparna Mohanty is also a significant voice of this period. Though her poems are sometimes brutally frank about sex or sexuality, they never try to get closer to highly personal Confessional poetry, which talks about abortion, menstruation, incest and adultery, etc.

Some of the most important poets of the late '70s are Prasanna Kumar Patasani, Ashutosh Parida, Aswini Kumar Mishra, Pradeep Biswal and Satya Pattanaik; they all wrote astonishing poems of rare beauty, depth and complexity of thought together. They tried their hand at writing a kind of poetry that could be subtle, thoughtful, and carefully constructed. Pradeep is a versatile poet; and neo-romantic in spirit, he never allows gloom or despair to rule over his poetic world. He loves life too much; he can always entertain his readers with a smile. Aswini, who is the most prolific of all, writes on a variety of themes. Though at times he sounds expressly ideological in his thoughts and expressions, his work can be best understood in terms of his romantic responses to the objects or things around him. The early poetry of Patasani was deeply concerned about human suffering; his concerns had deep echoes of Marxist ideology and thoughts. He was one of the leaders of the Progressive Movement in Odia poetry. But the real progressive spark came from Rabi Singh and Brajanath Rath, who believed in the complete relationship between art and society. Rabi can be best described as a Leftist who raised a hellfire to destroy social ills like inequality, discrimination and violence which were rampant in the day's society. Satya Pattanaik is a diaspora poet who is currently based in the United States of America. Torn between the two worlds, the one he has left far behind and the other he lives now as an immigrant, Satya writes mostly on conflicts of cultural duality, nostalgic reminiscences and painful sense of loss and uprootedness in the country he has adopted. In the poem "Immigrant" he tries to capitalize on the experience of an immigrant, who makes an incredible contribution to the prosperity of the country he has embraced as a matter of choice.

Hrushikesh Mallick chose the rural people and life, even their language as the most perfect material for poetry. His poetry reminds one of the Chinese "farmstead poetry" in which the poets use rural matters and setting as theme of their creativity. It is not known whether Hrushikesh writes from personal experience of the village or sympathetic observation of the rustic simplicity over urban sophistication. In his poetry. Ajay Pradhan, a poet from the pilgrim city of Puri, uses *Puri boli,* a typical language which the temple servitors and the city's original inhabitants use in their daily conversation. Satrughna Pandab and Senapati Pradyumna Keshari are remarkable poets. Pradyumn's *Putana,* a collection of forty-one poems, as a matter of fact, sequences, heralded a return to the tradition of long-poems, after the form was popularized by Guruprasad Mohanty in "Kalapurusha" and Sitakant Mahapatra in *Astapadi.*

At the turn of the century, the Odia poetry which mostly banked upon complexity, wit and imagery took to a different mode of expression. The new poets tried to bring poetry into people's lives by writing a kind of poetry, which according to Philip Larkin, one "can understand first go: easy rhythms, easy emotions, easy syntax." There is no denying that these poets have tried to woo the readers, even those readers who might not feel poetry is for them. I have included poets who are born post-1960, at least a decade after India made her tryst with destiny. By the time these poets came to poetry writing in the late nineties even later, the aftermath of independence was not something for them to reckon with. Most of us writing at least thirty years before they were following in the tradition of modern poetry, initiated by Sachi Rautray and Ramakanta Rath. But then the number of people who wrote was less than what it is today. Today, poetry seems to be everywhere, including in literature festivals. There is an alarming boom of literary festivals organized by certain individuals who manage to garner corporate support for their high budget festivals. This new trend of corporate literature might not be helpful to the genuine poets as the organizers are more focused on power and position through which they can mint money.

Yet, I find hundreds of young poets writing in the new vein; and some of them are writing really amazing poetry. As I read them, I am really impressed by the way they strive after some degree of lucidity and clarity of expression, the economy of words and precision of language, besides their mesmerizing imagery. The 'Next Generation' poets as I call them, have the potential to lead the change in the coming years. I hope the poets like K.Shyamababu Dora, Gayatribala Panda, Bijayalaxmi Parida, Amiya Ranjan Mahapatra will dominate Odisha's poetic landscape of the coming years if things go well. I do not say they are the best of the emerging poets; there are still some others like Sitanshu Lenka, Ipsita Sarangi, Sharmistha Sahoo, Sushri Sangita Mishra, Narendra Kumar Bhoi, Manini Mishra and Runu Mohanty, who are writing really fantastic poetry, but I cannot include them all for lack of space here. They all write audaciously simple verse, the verse which can steal hearts, feed minds with new ideas and thoughts. I have translated only those who I think are the best to represent almost a hundred years of Odia poetry in the English-speaking world.

Without translation, we would be living in provinces bordering on silence.

- Professor George Steiner

CONTENTS

Sachi Routray	25
Binod Chandra Nayak	27
Guruprasad Mohanty	29
Bhanuji Rao	31
Chintamani Behera	33
Rabi Singh	35
Uma Shankar Panda	37
Ramakanta Rath	39
Sarat Chandra Pradhan	41
Brahmotri Mohanty	42
Kamalakant Lenka	44
Bibek Jena	46
Jagannath Prasad Das	49
Bibhudatta Mishra	50
Brajanath Rath	54
Sitakant Mahapatra	56
Deepak Mishra	58
Sourindra Barik	59
Soubhagya Kumar Misra	61
Nityanand Pati	63
Nityanand Nayak	65
Banshidhar Sarangi	67
Harihar Mishra	68
Prasanna Kumar Mishra	70
Saroj Ranjan Mohanty	72
Dillip Das	74
Pramod Kumar Mohanty	75
Praharaj Satyanarayan Nanda	76
Niranjan Padhi	78
Phani Mohanty	80
Rajendra Kishore Panda	83
Nilamani Parida	86
Haraprasad Das	87
Gopalakrushna Rath	90

Nrusingh Prasad Tripathy	92
Prativa Satapathy	94
Prasanna Kumar Patasani	96
Ashutosh Parida	98
Devdas Chhotray	101
Mamata Dash	102
Baikunthanath Sahoo	104
Sarojoni Sarangi	106
Amaresh Patnaik	108
Manorama Biswal Mahapatra	109
Soubhagyabant Maharana	111
Bhagaban Jayasingh	113
Aparna Mohanty	115
Aswini Kumar Mishra	117
Haraprasad Parichha Pattanaik	119
Hrushikesh Mallick	121
Pravasini Mahakud	123
Shatrughna Pandab	125
Amarendra Khatua	126
Prasanna Kumar Mohanty	127
Binapani Panda	129
Pitambar Tarai	131
Senapati Pradyumna Keshari	133
Pradeep Biswal	135
Surya Mishra	137
Kamal Kumar Mohanty	139
Ajay Pradhan	141
Satya Pattanaik	143
Rakshak Nayak	145
Sunil Kumar Prusty	147
Sucheta Mishra	149
Amiya Ranjan Mohapatra	151
Suresh Nayak	153
K. Shyamababu Dora	155
Swapna Mishra	157
Sharmistha Sahoo	159
Kedar Mishra	161
Manoj Kumar Meher	163
Bijayalaxmi Parida	165
Gayatribala Panda	167
Contributors	169

Sachi Routray
PRATIMA NAYAK

The pale moon in the sky white as foam
has struck a deal between light and darkness.

At a distance, a chimney continues to cough on its own
The 8 O'Clock mail rumbled by the Dhansiri river.

Just then a brahminy duck moans as penned in poetry
when I bumped into Pratima Nayak after many long days.

With pimple-scarred face she held a leather bag in hand
Her dull cheeks bloomed futility
of unpretentious scars.

Her body sick from diseases, face scarred by pimples
The loose, pale-flame like the body wrapped in khaki cloak.

Dust of age had covered her body pretty as bougainvillea
And I asked her, How are you? My voice had a ring of sorrow.

Pratima smiled where the blue skyline
touched the ochre edge of the earth
There -
beyond the confluence of dream and reality
we stood together
The long two-year-old world was asleep behind us
yes, a world of just two years
ash-grey, hazy, horrendous, ravaged by war.

Far off a hurricane lamp flickered in the mortuary.
Appallingly,
it sent fear and fear all around.

Her nuptial bond was in wreck.
She was studying MA in Philosophy.
Maybe she had fallen in love once or twice.

Loss of father, weight of debt,
conspiracy galore:
They all had put an end to her study-
MA in philosophy.

Again nineteen-forty
wiped out whatever was left behind
she took refuge in the Department of Supplies, though
her wage was not bad.
That is how it gave an identity to her.

Pratima Nayak smiles
Her lips bear the hints of a dream.
A khaki smile on her face, her eyes having
hints of the night
two momentous forests on both her sides
the stars rushing in streams.

Ah, let Pratima Nayak smile
Her saree has no anchal,
she is clad in khaki only.

∎

Binod Chandra Nayak
A SOLITARY MILEPOST

This sky is blue as love
green as grass
Or the storm has turned green
in love for grass.
The solitary milepost
Prickly
The name goes wrong
Where is Subhadra's home?

Poisonous,
red sandalwood-colored mushroom,
very black maggots,
And caterpillar
who after shedding its skin
transforms into a butterfly
a fairy of the fairy world
And Satyavati
who after wiping off the smell of fish
spreads out her fragrance for miles.

Perched on the same milepost
A little bird in yellow
reads out poetry of the branches

and of clouds in Bhim Pallishree
The pearls of memory
Stretch over miles
How alas they are all gone now
The palanquin passed this way
to the beats of *telengi*
in the scorching summer heat
Even if Lavanya Dei, Kalavati
or Radha Damayanti who had gone this way
have not returned as yet
to see things in tears once again.

The bird flew away
wiping off the smiles of the milepost
on the wings of dreams
The shadows continue to return
like the memories of love.

Guruprasad Mohanty
THE DOVES OF MY EYES

Striking against the sky's steel body
the doves of my eyes
return to this earth where you
wait for me alone to grasp the meaning
of sickness, death and life again.

When the sea waves coax
the motionless sands with their little hands,
I seek the ancestral memories
in your indolent flesh running through
the hot grey afternoon.
You tell, tell the secrets of leaf and grass,
the story of the woods and cliff,
of moss and shells, the story of the sea
and of the desolate moon
among the rumpled clouds in
a gloomy night drifting away
to their death on the other side.

You glean the sinking body of chaitra
among the little whirlpools of sand
you also love and call out holding my hand
where is your soul? where is my body alive?
when the doves of your mind
strike against the steel body of the sky.

And when my mind's dove comes back
crossing over the sky's illusions
the river of time flows past my dreams
through the weariness of your body,
the furor of hunger, sighs and sorrow.

I cannot hear the fall of leaves
in the quiet noon, the breath of the sun,
the forest of casuarinas melts into
the sky as smoke
I cannot recollect when the doves of my eyes
could discover you in the downtown Cuttack
        or Ujjain.

Bhanuji Rao

HEART

Heart breaks heart
It is a deadly weapon
not seen anywhere
in the world.

Heart is like
a suicidal bomb
First it slaughters the self
then others.

Heart is like a river
If it swallows a chunk of its bank
It also builds up a mass of land
somewhere
If a landslide destroys a home
it creates an island elsewhere.

A churning heart
makes a summer palm bloom
Only a heart understands
the language of heart
There is no need of
the tremors of eyelids
Or the delicate explosions of lips.

Sometimes suddenly
heart burns the heart
It turns the golden life to ash
when I feel I should bury
this burnt out heart under the ash.
Let this heart sink to sleep
till eternity.

Chintamani Behera
A PRAYER BEFORE DEATH

Tortured all through my life
I want to die now, this moment.
Yes I want to die at your feet, O God!
If you are my soul
You can save me by your magic hand
By the powers of your art or magic.
(Is that true?
Or, an exciting belief of man?)

I want to die
As a witness on the opposite party
To put forward all that untrue and unfeeling
In your court of law
But when as Asutosh, you get easily cajoled
By your devotees
How can I hope for justice
The words of conscience
Eternal and Beautiful
Which are but true in all ages.

Please therefore listen
To my ultimate helpless wails
If after death I turn into a flute
I must sing the song
of joy, ecstasy and dream,
The unrhymed voice of the morning
Or a mother's hot tears for her child
The sprouts of love, amity and passion
That will become not only for me
but for you as a deathless creation
A manifestation of Aum.

■

Rabi Singh
SELF-INFLICTION

Nothing has been left out for survival
All around bodies of men are burning on pyre
Heaps of slur and insult growing by days
How long should I read the Gita of deception?

Torn between life and death
The poet cannot know where he has to land
He cannot either burn in the flame
or quench the fire
The Grand Time bursts into wild laughter.

Greatly bruised my body and soul
My poetry gets raped in broad daylight
Yet, the day cannot come to its dead end
My poetry reflects the hunter who killed the bird.

Those who had conquered death are all dead
I am sitting with hands folded over the eyes
The sorrow-ridden past trembles to say
You have no possibility, nothing.

I cannot see the face of future
The limitless cries all look blurred
Devastatingly burns fire of self-centeredness
That has already gripped the human world.

Inside or outside everywhere stalk the animals
Exploitation, torture or extortion continue to hit
Let the sky and earth be one
Let the earth stop its celestial journey.

Farewell O Earth, fallen you Witch
Desecrated stand your body and soul
You are but a massive mound of sin
I am dying in repentance hitting my cheeks
With shoes.

Uma Shankar Panda
RHYTHM OF THE DAWN

Winter, spring or monsoon
dazed moonlight or distraught darkness
the lilt of the fiery flute of dawn--
they all permeate every space
and the body. Merchant' wife
is shining brightly in an unknown ship
in the midst of many-splendored sapphires
the song of the sea swans
creates the sad music
of *jaltarang*.

If sometimes the morning clouds
bear the alphabets of spring
the other time they feel
the exciting romance of winter
The tryst of words
are like the sleep-laden star flowers
Lonely and eternal time
stands face-to-face with time
which has no companion.

Are you in the dream-filled world of
Chagall, Cezanne, Van Gogh or Picasso
Where are you?
Are you in the company of Bilhan,
Banabhatta or Vatsyayan?
A restless sorrow that you are
You lie in bed in silence like
an abandoned saree in sorrow
on the ever-stretching sea beach
smelling of evening.

Are you not a new love poem either of
Rajendra or Ramakanta
Once I read then I feel as though
I have been reading you
all through the night or all through the season
Lifelong.
when the parting of your hair
vermilion looks bright
and the grand time shivers through your lips.

Your body like the red glowing *palash*
hued by the season's mirth
rings like a crackle in my blood
for light years, through thousand dawns.

You are the Devi of all my beings
I am the flute of Brahman
like a wordless sound of Om.
■

Ramakanta Rath

SRI RADHA
(An Excerpt)

When you touched me for the first time

all the emptiness within me
reverberated with sound
It seemed you called me from all directions
for what I could have become
from their longing.

That voice had no sound
You did not even speak a word,
Yet, it seemed you called me in a loud voice
louder than the sound of the seven seas;
with the roar of thunder
the booms of earthquake
you have demolished my forms
and their transformations
asking me to become what
I have always longed to be.

When I hid myself behind
my several roles
and articulated all their thoughts
as though I believed in what they said
and went on describing
like the memorized dialogues
the smallest of small things
like the milk and the curd I sold
like my very small dilemmas
and very small longings.

Sometimes I felt
Even more limited was my youth
that had lost its fire
Someday, I might forget the moment
you touched me for the first time
and look at the *kadamba* trees
in blossoms which wilted
when the river glowed in moonlight.

Still I knew
when you touched me for the first time
today or tomorrow, or maybe some other day
I'll give you a gift of my willingness
I'll relapse into silence
and during the course of a single night
would become something
that I always wished to be
I would embrace you for all times to come
in the stark nakedness of my inner self.

■

Sarat Chandra Pradhan
THREE PRAHARAS

Morning: A smile lurks on
             the lips of a girl
             Smeared in turmeric
             her fair body sparkles
             after a bath.

Noon: The woman looks
             morose
             as though her face
             is a livid ember.
             A flight of pigeons
             coo although her body
             flying from sky to sky.

Evening: The old woman
             with sunken eyes
             gropes all the way
             sharpening her mind
             grins in the depository
             of *jahni* blossoms.

■

*In ancient India, Prahar (a Sanskrit term), was considered to be a unit of time, or subdivision of the day, approximately three hours long. The day is divided into eight parts: four praharas for the day, and four for the night.

Brahmotri Mohanty
STRANGE DESIRES

In moments of an intense desire
I wish: You should fling me into the air
like a ball
and by stretching your arms
clasp me when squealing in excitement
I begin to fall on the ground.

Or, on the bank of a river,
pretending to show me its blue water
you could push me into its water
and then pluck me from there
when in shock and awe with my eyes closed
I could hold you tight
In the dense cloudless autumn.

I am no longer interested to listen to
your sweet words of love in solitude;
Or keeping my head on your chest
enjoy the thrill of a sparkling moonlight.
I would like to feel
the unbounded awe in joy.

Down with numbness, my soul
is bored with perfunctory love;
I wish to taste the wanton love in terror
My heart is stoked and forehead
is flooded with jasmines of sweat
Even though it is ingrained in
something like lies and sin.

For God's sake,
Please keep my request.
or else I will call you a coward,
a eunuch, cruel and merciless.

Kamalakant Lenka

HOW I AM LIVING

Who says I am living?
If living is breathing
counting waves or swimming in the waters
or quarrelling with the self
Then, who says I am living?

If living is to glean wanton words
from the furtive glances
steal colors from the lips
expel mindlessness from the mind
put a strip of bandage on the wound
cull out mustard seeds from the sands
or wave a cane to flaunt authority
then who says I am living
who says I do not drink water
I do not swim in the river
count the waves
gulp down a morsel of food.

If living means to join hands to clap,
pluck out flowers, wash the clothes,
apply hair dye to the beard
why then revelry grips
the solitary *dak* bungalow
trivial assumes an unanswered seriousness
who says I am living
who says I have forgotten meaning of evil
the unwavering simplicity of virtue.

The meaning of living is to spew
sandal paste on the moist carpet
The sly arrogance of fake dreams
who say then I am living
and nodding my head
to every word you speak
agreeing to everything without logic
keeping mum and smiling!!

■

Bibek Jena

THE VOICE

1.
Stretch your hand towards
the secret and lovesome darkness
I will put my head on your lap
and cry in the ultimate hour.

I am a storehouse of cries
of desperation underlying my blood
when for the last time
fear grabbed me in the solitary night.

Please come under
the ultimate spell of a moonless night
in the silent fragrance of
your disheveled hair to wipe out
some drops of tears after
I spoke my final words in the exciting throbs

of your wet eyelids;
Please stretch out your hands
towards my ultimate pain.

2.
The night will end today.
Also all nights of many known
and forsaken darkness
the past adorned with many
painful memories
the story of the past of all languages
the aroma of many secret nights
the throbs of many longings.

Before this last night of
painful pain comes to an end
Please light the last lamp of
all secret memories
and bid me farewell through
the warmth of your last tears.

3.
Thinking of me as a dense block
of darkness
Or, maybe you thought of stealing
a chunk of sleep
When you came you never imagined
that lightning could suddenly irradiate the darkness
and darkness could burn with all the radiance
with memories' fuel.

Now see all the burning
has come to a dead end
The one who burnt and the one
who made him burn
You and I on the bank of a river
or on the burial ground
or, on a *peepal* branch, in the wind,
and very intense darkness
inner silence calls both of us
Please hold my hand, I'm scared.
∎

Jagannath Prasad Das
BIDDING FAREWELL

At the time of bidding farewell
nothing is left unattended to
Like a wretched man
who has no intention to scream
when he drowns in the mid-ocean.

The man bidding adieu thinks
how love was different from loving
how life was different from living
how far was the song from singing!

The drowning man thinks
and surrenders
while searching for the sea
as different from the waves
he keeps himself aloof from bidding adieu
The drowning man.

Bibhudatta Mishra
AGNAATAVAS

When shall the disguise of the Pandavas come to an end?
Flinging away my mask
I shall rise again
The earth will shudder to hear my proud footsteps;
A storm will brew in the sea
The earth, the sky and the nether world
will shake in fright
panting for breath.

In my arrival
the flower-bride will hide
among the dark foliage in awe
out of Rudra's anger
the twang of the shooting arrows
will silence all commotions of the earth,
and the mad tunes of music and dance.

Do not know how long shall I have to
spend in disguise as Brihannala
among the women forgetting
the utter joy of battle?

Driven by a mad desire
I feel like embracing the nearby *shami* tree
where lies the passion of my soul,
Throw away this mask
without fear and fright,
no matter if I have to go through
yet another period of exile in the forest
which is a hundred times better
than concealing my real self
the alphabets of my life
my ruthless manhood, livid as lava,
It's better than yielding at their feet.

No longer do I love to wear
my hairs in plaits
enjoy a reading of songs
the rhythm of music and dance
No no, forgetting the fields out
in the distance
searching for the arrows
on the breasts of the foes.

My life is on fire, the tongue of flame
burning with rapid breaths
that can destroy the world
engulfing pavements, the seven seas
and the distant skies with ferocity galore.
This life in *agnaatvas*
I do not like at all
in these narrow and dingy environs
under this shrunken and lifeless sky.

I do not like to spend life
like a widow with a thin and frail body
on this lonely and desolate riverbed
Here I can only hear
the incoherent dialogues,
frightful shrieks, painful cries of women
the obscene waves of pagan joy
the wild laughter of flattery
the dance of fancy among the courtiers.
No longer have I the face of a warrior
my companion of the battle, the horse,
the chariot, the dreaded weapon
Who has taken away all these
in this period of disguise?

I am a distant tornado
that can devour like a horrendous storm
My identity does not reflect
peace, a mild, sweet and timorous smile
lifeless and morose
only a mask of my *agnaatvas*.

Who knows how many days are left
for me to complete the *agnaatvas*?
Who knows?
When will it end?
life's spiteful, ignoble phase
This tornado will find its way
to ravage with wild ferocity panting
at a ferocious speed

the pent-up anger will burst into
hundreds of cyclones
When shall this phase of *agnaatvas*
come to an end?

∎

Brihannala: The poem is a monologue; it comes out of the lips of Brihannala who finds mention in the Hindu epic Mahabharata. Arjuna had assumed this name to spend one year of his exile at the palace of King Virata. He taught song and dance to Princess Uttara in the disguise of a eunuch. Brihannala stayed at the palace for women, moving about and making friends with other maids and princess' friends. No one could suspect that Brihannala the eunuch was indeed the great hero of the Mahabharata.

Brajanath Rath
MANOHARPUR

It was midnight
when the hands of a half-burnt clock
had stopped
in incredible cruelty
and where the ongoing, distant time
had relapsed into silence
Do you know the name of that village?
It's Manoharpur.
--- --- ---
This tribal hamlet stands here
nestled among the forests and hills
Who has christened this village?
Such a wonderful name!
Today there is a Takshak around
to sting with his secret, demoniac fang,
And the little doe of fear-stung humanity
has fallen down stung by the serpent
when trying to run helter skelter.
--- --- ---
The ashen flag of
the so-called custodians of dharma
is unfurled in the naked sky

when the blind horizon returns
the mad echoes of their outcry of joy
The moon in its fifth lunar phase
looks pale in shame
The cold dews of the winter end
fall broken down in sorrow.

--- --- ---

Manoharpur
is no more the same Manoharpur as before
as if it has turned dumb
and lost her virgin innocence
after the beastly rape by a coward.

--- --- ---

The rape-hurt humanity
is engulfed in the gruesome fire here
which is still raging with all its atrocity,
Will the horn-mad flames
of religious violence
be extinguished or not?

■

Sitakant Mahapatra
LOVE SONG OF A DHANGRA

On a hill-slope
I asked you to give me love, dream,
a touch and tobacco leaves
You said, so many *podu*-farmers
are here around
Not here.

In the evening darkness
at the end of an unquiet village
under the fragrance of *mahula* blossoms
I asked you to give me love, your body
or else, give me words
You said, I'm always scared of
glow-worms and lonely stars
It's better to run away from this solitary place.

In the dense forest where one could hear
the throbs of one's own heart
I asked you to give me love, a touch
You said, O No,
here the earth is pale and grey
My body is like a flower, my soul
sparkles as gold

Would not they wilt under cover of dust?
Not here, not here.

There was none on the bank of a rivulet
except for a lonely bird trilling
I asked you to give me a touch and darkness
You said, everything looks bright in
the mirror of the rivulet's pellucid waters
Not here, not here.

The whole world went back to sleep
even the moon and the stars
I asked to give me a touch, your life
for my fluttering soul
I asked you for a chunk of place
in the nest of your body
You said, I could see in the mirror of your eyes
everything looks lucent
Not now, not now.

I could gouge out my two eyes,
and offering them like lotus flowers
I said, take, and now give me a touch,
love and darkness
Give me some balm for my ulcerated soul.
∎

Deepak Mishra
RUUK

Wife demands blood and flesh
Son asks for wealth
Ladylove claims rest of my mind
My body demands a position equivalent to
Those of a palanquin and flowers.
Bones have urged me
For their immersion
In the waters of Prayag or Gangotri
Ego is committed to
Find in Amaravati a place for itself.

What can I give you
My entire wealth is limited to
A handful of clean and deep silences
Which I have plucked out
From... your stream
O Chitrotpala
From your deep dee blue sanctum sanctorum.
∎

Sourindra Barik

SHAKUNI

Desperate Shakuni that I am:
On the heaps of skeletons
I have seen
the limits of my world;
The wall of Duryodhan
has encircled me
My heart is under fire
my hand has a piece of bone
my father's.

Those who gifted me
their age
by cutting their own
Their droplets of blood
my mind soaked
I swear to wipe out that blood
with Kaurav's.

Hence the chivalry.
the pellet drum of a lost religion.
Bhagirath invites
the fountain of blood.

The house of lacquer is burnt
the dice go on rolling
my bones move crashing
Draupadi gets disrobed
in Kaurav's court.

Kurukshetra or Dharmakshetra
of my dreams
is the fruit of my penance
my kith and kin
the door to my salvation
The waters of the Ganges
the scarlet river
at their sorrowing face.

Sahadev!
I have played enough with my father's bone
The fire of my eyes has burnt me enough
my sarcastic laughter at the Kaurav's court
The dream of a Dharmakshetra
burns like a river of blood
I have died enough, yes enough,
The pain of hell has consumed me enough.

Therefore you Shahadev
Kill me
My ultimate victory is death
Casting aside the dice
the waters of the Ganges
arrived now.

∎

*In the Mahabharata, Shakuni is painted as main villain by Sage Vyasa Dev. He was the brother of Gandhari and maternal uncle of Duryodhana.

Soubhagya Kumar Misra

A TALE OF THE MONKEY AND THE CROCODILE

Why did you choose me to be your friend
when there were so many animals around you
Didn't you notice a deer, a fox,
a flock of grazing goats, or rats and rabbits?
Is it that your hands and feet did not move
you could not see things properly?
You had already become old when I knew you.

It's true that I was in the possession of a berry tree
there was a need to find shelter from the rain and the sun
this life is like a bubble
should I make you understand more?

Why did you choose me for this misery when there were
so many animals around?
Now it's the season of rains
ripe berries aplenty
you'll not come to ask for berries
do you have a face to ask for
once you have begged for my liver
after being cheated?

Of course you have been cheated, still
I cannot say for sure someone
might not get my liver again
After once you begged for it
it remained as your own till eternity?
Did you ask for being your own?

Why did I go riding on your back
I knew it was a fathomless depth
a simple turn might have devastated
my world
how did you bring me back
Is the trust yet another name for mistrust?
Or there is nothing called trust or mistrust?
till we belonged to two different worlds
you to the waters and I to the twigs.

We have tasted one defeat each
and one victory each
I have to stay in happiness
yet, last night a crow went on cawing
that disturbed me whole night
I can see you come swimming
your tail sparkling like silver
I am bleeding within
Has the time come to pin a trust
on each other for the last time?
And suspect each other?
I cannot jump down
Take me along with the tree.

Nityanand Pati
DEATH

Death turns out to be history
After attainment of moksha
Can death have the complete
and empty experience of its own?
Again death pursues stealthily
on the archway of darkness
in its first attempt through irritation and futility;
Is the *Baikuntha* any better than
the love-sodden sky and the moon?
Are life and youth ignoble on the ladder
of death?
Is joy in creation closer to me than
my own happiness?
Can one listen to the song of a flute
in God's *Anantashayan*?
The dismal darkness dispels away
the difference between the others
and my own.

O Death!
You are the silent music of all pretensions
Your voice rings a tune of deep attachment
that torments the fulcrum of this creation
Maybe I have seen you in
some distant mountains
or in the ultimate flicker of a lamp
where the heart slowly burns
either in deadly *baisakha*
or at the fag-end of *chaitra*.

■

Nityanand Nayak

BIRDS: THE NIGHT OF THE MOON

1.

In the sky the flock of birds look like
a circular garland of flowers
Sometimes they fly in curves
Or run straight in a line
breaking midway to join again
in a strange fashion
Like a wife's misunderstanding.

The bird,
that like an innocent child's self-confidence
deftly flying the kite,
flies in the sky
As though it's a love letter
which the wind carries
with the sighs of separation.

A pristine night of the moon
descends down upon the earth
In the songs of birds
In the fragrance of the mango blossoms
Or in the ragas as Megh Malhar
and Basant-Kedar
flowing through the breath
in the body's smell.

2.

Here, down below
Against the backdrop of death and time
lies the bed of grass,
The terrace of ripe paddy fields
The flight of joyous birds over the vortex
their endless twitters
Like those of picnicking schoolboys.
The exquisite nest of agile bird
that excites their cheeping little ones
with blue dreams to build a nest
beyond all sorrows or obstacles
which prevent them from flying away
from themselves.

■

Banshidhar Sarangi
THE SUNDOWN

The front door was open
There was no one in the adjacent room
All that I could hear was the footfall of the wind
and the cries of the dead leaves.

Through the window I could see
a dry deodar tree
a flock of dead parrots perched on it
The sunrays went on lengthening
in the house and courtyard
There is none in the house
Where have they all gone?

Let them go wherever they like
But the deodar is dead
The parrots have perished
The evening continues to squat on
the dry deodar tree
when Manorama is seated
with her hair disheveled and eyes dry
and indifferent
which burn out everything they see.

Once again she is pregnant
she is ready to make her son a yogi
with a begging bowl in hand
No one will speak a word about it.

Harihar Mishra
THE UPROOTED

Being uprooted
The lotus moves ahead
as it playfully slips away
from the hand.

How can I hold it back
to save the lotus from the clutch of sludge
or from the jaws of a croc?
Why should I worry
or say a prayer
If a wave drifts away over my head
one after the other
even if we live for a day
by cancelling out
poison with poison?

No crisis will pop up any more
even if we push our head
into yet another crisis?

It is impossible
to fare forward
unless the lotus does not move
and coax all our hopes and dreams
of the Uprooted;
Perplexed still in conflict
stands here the polished floor
of the sea beach.
■

Prasanna Kumar Mishra
IN SPRING'S OWN HOUSE

The other day you, I and Amrataru
all three were together in
spring's own house.

The fragrance of mango blossoms
wafted into the environs
A mad excitement
stuck around the stunted twigs.

I could see how I was beginning
to bloom like you bloomed
in seasons or no-seasons.

It was the first caress of spring
when she stepped into our world
like a guest
and then became easy and familiar
as breath.

I placed my wearisome life
on your open palm
but with a drop of tear you
made it placid and tranquil.

Spring knew the art how to
mollify the crabby
with a rare kiss of contentment
and tame the restless with a restful ease
you had learnt the art from spring.

After I freed myself from
a maze of streets
I could discover myself on your lap
as a tamed hoodless cobra
spring had wiped out all the fear
from your mind.

I could not speak as before
the language of treachery
known to our ancient texts
the day you embraced
spring for the first time
why are you so spunky about it!

Every squabble might
hurt the spring outside the window
so I assured her with an offer
of my life, yet you never sulked
to offer a palmful of breasts to me.

Thank you Amrataru.
You are there because of spring
who has spread its fragrance in glee
Thank you spring
I was never tired of kissing
beauty's bounties.

■

Saroj Ranjan Mohanty
THE REMAINDERS

There is something
One has to gain and lose in life:
If sometimes it spawns new dreams
The other time
It shreds into thousand splinters
As it plays the game of loss and gain
Life's additions and subtractions
Through its ceaseless movement
Lifelong.

At the end of all subtractions
The leftovers are only the life's
Assets which one leaves behind
As he departs bidding
Adieu to the world.

With a multiplier
And multipliables,
Life dabbles in life's ebullience,
The rapture of creation
As the capital gain, life's
Rich dividends.

Multiplication is not
Life's game ultimate
There still waits
The hide and seek of divisions
The inexorability of
Dividing the self
And life's all assets.

The game rips the man
Splits his profile,
his ecstasy of love
Empathy and affection
Though what remains ultimately
Are the remainders
One's repayment towards living
Despite odds.

It has been my dream
My sadhana to leave behind
As much remainders
Before my eyes are closed.

■

Dillip Das

DEMOCRACY

The bright white rabbits
are only
the messengers of God.

They live on
green grass and leaf.

With their
bright black eyes
they get lost
in forest greenery.

But
O! what fools are they!

They surrender themselves
without being aware
of it
again and again.

In the forest
of sovereignty
they live like epiphytes
fill the bellies of
sly and crafty men.

Pramod Kumar Mohanty
THE FLOOD

Your irresistible foot might come
Crashing into the solid foundation
Of my pucca house
When the white body of a dead calf
sparkles in the thousand grins
of a god of dharma.

Life begins to sink slowly after you come.

You are only an unbroken
and intimate cry that spreads
beyond the horizon like water
and which appears as a god in
every being in silence, every moment.

Death is a silent physician
who always arrives late in a boat
in such a way that he remains
half-hidden like a rainbow
or like the half-narrated tale
of a village companion.

At the end of the therapy
a black drongo comes flying
alone
to perch on the thatch of thin bamboo sticks.

Praharaj Satyanarayan Nanda
GEOMETRY OF THE SUN

Every sunrise brings in
the translucent rays of the mind
The rest remains on the bed
As a belief in the life we lead,
When the red buds on the railings
Begin to shake like the two arms
Raised in humble suppliance.

There is no bottled-up brightness
Yet, the sun with its tender touch
Washes clean the rest of the mind
Pouring out dreams and spring
Like the drops of pearl on a pot of gold.

Am I living on a verandah
Or in front of a gate?
Your invite hangs from every branch
In the sounds of honey bees buzzing around
Which is yet to touch my soul.

Whether or not the fugitive mind comes
On the steps of the spirit
Which I have placed in between
A circular void
Your footsteps look like a child's fist
A small invite.

Through the window the sun gives off
the dust of its rays
The limitless compassion ingrained
In the last eye contacts
Returns like a fragrance of the first breath
What a tremendous invite it is!

Niranjan Padhi
THE HIEROGLYPHS OF AN ARTIST

Is not he the artist
who paints the germ-eaten liver
of a TB patient
and ties a bandage
on the pus-filled abscess of a leper?

He is the artist
who joins a magnolia bud
to its mother stem
and scratches out a new map of cosmos
through a string of words.

He is the artist
who seeks light in the dark
and makes poison taste as nectar;
one who descends down on earth
to slick with dust
or rise from the sea's womb
to glisten as a dew drop.

Is not he the artist
who digs out a sepulcher
to trace out life's seed
and sing paeans of love
in one's sorrow-stung life?

If the artist's creation
is the voice of my heart
Let that voice be the part
of a mighty being!

Phani Mohanty
THE LADYLOVE

After you went away
leaving me alone
I began to sink and sink
in the fathomless depth
of the mid-ocean.

There is no one around
to bear a hand-
life comes to a grinding halt.
I have become my own foe
and dying like a man
in the bottomless waters.

O my Ladylove
sorrow is a blue river
And sitting silently alone
on the sorrow-stifled river
I could see your pale face
on its rippled water
You are like a dense dapple of shadow
on my line of fate.

What is happening all around
and at whose behest, My Love,
I do not know why
mouth dries up, telephone goes dead
the smell of sulphur spreads
densely across the sky
each news is crammed with
the meaningless 42-alphabets.

Flabbergasted my heart
lives with all soft sweet words,
I live and die moment to moment
like some strange desire
of an un-worshipped Yogini
blighted with a curse.

Is it that nothing is happening
in our world?
Is there no hope in the world we live?
One day, suddenly the river of life
will overflow its banks
man's fate will change on its own
like the dappled wings of a *baramasi* bird.

Maybe some invisible cruel time
will print a cross on his own hand
and never return again
after he is gone.

Now I cannot cross the crossroad
despite my every effort, My Love,
Will you then clasp my brown body
crumpled and thin with age

Will you wipe off the drops of sweat
from my forehead with your
milk white scarf
and narrate a new story

forgetting about all the ills of the past
when an untimely rain
will melt away
the frozen sorrows and pain.

Rajendra Kishore Panda

I MIGHT BE ARRESTED ANY MOMENT FROM NOW

I might be arrested any moment from now
For sedition
Democracy might turn the street singers
Into an armed force.

I might be dismissed any moment from now
For the crime of being indifferent
To the sovereign
For pronouncing eyes are not blue.

The eternal demon in me always
Abjures the fairies' signals
in the congregation of gods in heaven
I might be shot down for treachery
While asking for my equal rights
In the share of nectar.

Democracy might administer
electric shock to kisses
While embracing an iron statue of Bhima
Or maybe Dhritarashtra's replica of bones
Which might crash clattering into
thousand pieces.

It is better to tolerate the silence
In conversation with poetry
But, I do not want a bilingual identity
I don't need it, please don't force it upon me.

After I assumed the sky to be a flag
How can I show my fidelity
To some other flag?

With an express courage
I have embezzled away all silences
To form a word now
To return everything at a cumulative rate.

Yet
A pair of handcuffs will be made for me
In the blacksmith's workshop
After they melted away all creations
Only for me.

I might be arrested any moment from now
I might be exiled to a world of exile
I might be identified from the sign
of a bone-crossed skull
I might be punished for not

Calling myself a 'citizen'
For the horrific crime in claiming myself
to be a 'man.'

For the treason of saying 'I might be arrested any moment from now'
I might be arrested any moment from now
Suddenly…

Democracy might transform a mistrust
Into an incident.
∎

Nilamani Parida
PADMAKESHARIPUR VILLAGE

The other day A hundred-petalled rose
that had bloomed on
the squashy valley
of Padmakesharipur
has melted under
the sizzling summer heat.

The lamp of the sun
has been blown out;
in the distant horizon
the lonely stones
have dissolved into the blue.

The village girls
the crossway between
their heart and soul
shudders for a loaf of bread.
Sir, have you seen
how a deep and dense sigh
comes out of the lotus's heart?

Now the flame of poison
emanating from the blood and breath
has engulfed
the village of Padmakesharipur.
■

Haraprasad Das

THE INFINITE

I never think about death
I am not able to think
that a little while ago
those who went away bidding us adieu
will not come back at all.

With a red mark
on her round face that little girl
who danced on the ground grinning;
that old man who felt breathless
coughing endlessly after
he came back from the bank;
that young player-boy
who has come out of the field
after scoring a couple of goals--

I can never think that
they will never come back
they will surely come back
to the lap of darkness
with more luminance...

Now that little girl
must have grown up
and learnt the art of hiding
the cries in laughter;
that frail old man who is ready
to take a stroll out
with his copper-studded walking stick;
Unwary
that young vandal
must have come back to the base camp
tired
after he scaled some mountain.

Once they are gone
I cannot think
they will not come back at all.

After they are gone
a new road would emerge for each to tread
on the way back.
Or at least a new weapon
will be unsheathed somewhere
in the hands of a warrior
who spreads the fear of death
and there is none to resist.

They will come back,
come back for sure
to the lap of darkness
with more luminance
I have been waiting
with family of wife and son
for the Infinite.

It's because
I have no time to think about death
I cannot say it now
Even if I had time
I could never tell it to the neighbor
neighbor who has trespassed into my house,
I have already wrapped up
a deal with the Infinite.

Gopalakrushna Rath
FAREWELL TIME

I can hear someone's breath
on the desolate plain
which is so close to my heart!
Perhaps a new star is born
stretching endlessly
across an unimpeded sky.

It's dusk; the time for rest
has descended;
The satiated manhood
remains unhurt and composed.

Is it time to rake up sorrows?
Is it time to grope for the broken walls
of stolid empires?
When a hand stretches out
to hold a newborn
how unfair it is to squirm in pain
in the memory of a famine.

When I truly win a false battle
my opponents are lying dead
on their own courtyards;
He is a tired Abhimanyu whom I could have
surrendered my age
returning all the blessings at 9 O'clock
in the morning.

My destiny is such
Considering myself as a true companion
who promised to accompany me
through the desert sands
bumped into a rock statue
in anklets in the mid-desert
in a state of conflict, as always.

What a peaceful commotion
at this time of farewell
I can hear a voice of joy that comes
ringing from the mountain ranges
from miles-long forests
from beyond the oceans
The expression of a sweet welcome
The time of my farewell is so sweet
peaceful and expansive.

The garlands touching the feet
A sweet, tension-free footfall
when a sinless man slowly melts
into the horizon
towards the Invisible
stretching out both his hands in joy
breathing freely
with a heart to surrender...

At the time of farewell
At the time of farewell.
■

Nrusingh Prasad Tripathy

SEX

The house
after being thrown into disarray
by the first wind
slowly turns
into something
usual and in peace.

I knew
It was my first death
an empty place in the grand space
A momentary life
living inside an unbroken being.

From body to mind
and
from mind to super mind
from the earth to air
and
all extending non-wind
from love to compassion
then
absorption in samadhi.

SAMADHI

I raise the umbrella
as I wish
to escape the rain.
But the rain hardly bothers about
its own confines
The dark clouds along with the wind
spread across the forbidden caves
of my bones.

Peace is an alibi
like the umbrella.

My foot slips
on the moss of my incompetence.

A piece of bad news
has gone wild.

A hunter prowls now
inside the bazaar
on the neighbor's verandah
near a well
on the rectangular edge of woman's saree
drawing water
and on the lifeline of children
like the deep, dense bloody sighs
of a helpless man.

Prativa Satapathy
MY YOUNGEST SON

Again and again, at a slow pace,
as the new man descends from the void
I place at his feet
both the visible and the invisible
by stringing together the earth and the void
and turn myself into a bridge
of blood and flesh.

You shall come my dear child
I know, yes I know,
At the end, very late, after everybody else,
Was there anything left with me then?

The flesh would have been
chipped off the bone
the multi-hued butterfly would have flown
away from my lips' weak twigs
the brook of my breasts
would have gone dry
my lap would have looked empty
like a crumpled loaf of bread.

The *dho'baya* song
would be clung to the throat of
a way-laid traveler like a maze
the kajal-black forehead
would look like
the weather-beaten nest of a bird
that would have snapped from the tree
still I would be waiting
in the empty courtyard for you only.

Darkness would be hanging from
a leafy mango tree
like a dead buffalo
a ghastly chill would crowd into my feet
the honeybees would be feeling drowsy
in their hives.

You would come
your beautiful face sparkling
in the void like a bright moon
of the full moonlit night
But when I would hasten to embrace you, a
fragile bridge,
would have collapsed before your eyes.
■

Prasanna Kumar Patasani
OPEN MY EYES FOR ONCE

Open my eyes for once
I would like to see my dear river
how a lily blooms there
in my beloved's single drop of tear.

I long to see the blue hills
I long to see the distant mountains
how like my eyes
darkness encircles them there.

How the sun's ring fits
into the middle finger of the sky
I long to see the light's foot
and waves rolling on the sea.

The season is brimful of color it
it is ready to appear
in six snazzy apparels
but how can I see them
without a vision?

The pearls of dew that have fallen
on the lush green grass
which bear the alphabets of my heart
Please O God open my eyes for once
I would read them for sure.

I would see my beloved's face
like a blue moon rising
from a flurry of clouds of pain.

Beloved would be wearing ghagra
studded with little mirrors
in which I would be looking at my face
to her repeated laughter.

O God, open my eyes for once
It is not a great thing for you to do
I would love to see my beloved's face
a model of beauty and grace.
■

Ashutosh Parida

THE UNTOUCHABLE

I heard the name of hunger
from my mother's womb
saw it on my cradle
moved around as per its whim
beseeched:
"Oh my master, my mistress
scold me if you choose
give me work, give me rice
allow me to live like a pig
for my whole life."

With a piece of rock round my neck
I swim across the river
dig out the earth with nails
take a leap
from hunger to darkness
from darkness to hell
from hell to the sky
flying about
with the wings of hunger.

Locked up inside a seed
which has not germinated yet
the fragrance of my soul
has drifted away in the hot steam
like a horsewhip the shadow of food
has come flashing
on the branch of a fruit-laden tree
the aroma of rice has evaporated
from the embrace of sweat.

Who has given birth
to me and hunger?
Who has fastened
the horsewhip to hunger?
blood has dribbled down the forehead
I have flickered over that blood
I have eaten rice and whip
together.

I have drunk together
poison and faith
slept on the bed
of thorn and dew together
hunger is my voice
the tooth of a desert-
the roots of plants.

Hunger has no color,
yet it comes flowing into my eyes
the spectacle of red
someone pulls my tongue
towards the horizon
the ears can hear the sound
of the distant waterfall.

I roam the street
after ejecting from the belly
become one with the fire
after coming out of heart
chew the clay, the wind,
lick the light
swallow the sky.

I have known hunger from the womb
I can see my face
same as that of hunger.
■

Devdas Chhotray

ABSENCE

Do not throw
drops of your shining tears
to a wrong address.

I am no more here

Like the loathsome foot
of an ugly duck
I relax at the end of a street.

What is the use to prove
the story of a sparking shadow
the story of the river and the afternoon?

I am no longer here

I am burning here bright
like the festering wound of a tree
in a deep dense forest.

Mamata Dash
THE GUEST

I piled up life's all split-ups
to build the foundation of this house
all the pains to erect
the massive boundary around it.
All negligence and curses
turned into bricks and stone;
the roof was fashioned out
of iron rods of my wants and defeats.

The wall bore all the paints
of my sorrows and tears,
the chains of chores turned into
the wooden planks of my window
all my tireless labor
formed the household articles.

My incomplete love embellished
my garden with flowers and fruits,
It dolled up the green fountain of every
wound inside me;
all my failures and evil wishes
adorned like pictures
inside my house and outside;
all my sickness forged
different shades of light.

Deified,
my sense of freedom or attainments
appeared as gods
my hopes and aspirations
chimed melodious tunes.

Just then
I could hear a soft knock on my door
and as I opened it
I could see and recognize my guest
beyond my destiny
whom I was waiting for ages.

I was never prepared for this
How could I then believe
he would come here to my house?
■

Baikunthanath Sahoo
THE MIRROR

Mirror holds onto
the portrait of intimacy
that reflects an innocuous glance
a gesture of surrender.

Mirror chimes all
those words unspoken yet,
Mirror too remembers
poetry of life
engraved in sea sands
a tale of my joy
lurking on lips.

It maps out our
hundreds of unfulfilled desires
of a couple
Walking through winter chill
through rain and storm.

Please cancel poetry's life
Don't paint the places travelled
Don't stuff the mind's dialogues
into the drama of life
the anguish wet with tears,

But look into
the lonely and sweet moments
in a soft and tender state of joy.

Time is the other name of mirror
that helps life overflowing
with dreams, memories
tears and happiness.

Sarojoni Sarangi
CUTTACK

Today hundreds of candles
radiate the sky of your birth
hundreds of doves take to wings
with a message of love,
and dissolve into the somber grey sky.

Cuttack, my city of love,
my city of dreams
my city of memory
you are for me a city that glitters
like a piece of diamond.

The morning sunrays
as they touch your limbs
lazing around you
rise up like a silken girl
to erect an arch
of champak, jasmine and rose.

The Mahanadi and Kathajodi
have adored you with a necklace of gold
around your neck
the Barabati fort sparkles
like a diamond on your crown.

The temple conch blares
a divine tune
The Chandi temple reverberates
with evening prayer
Devi's bright mark of *sindoor*
illuminates devotees' faces.

Wherever I go I can feel
the throb of your vegetation
abundance of your wealth
of the entire world,
wherever you come
tearing through the fog
I can feel you with every touch.

On the pages of history
through years and ages
you shall continue to live
on the minds of the denizens
with flowers around
in the light of hundreds of candles.

I shall come back to you Cuttack
my City of Love,
from the banks of the rivers
fountains, forests and hills,
million times
I shall come back to you, to your lap
O my City of Dreams
like the first throb of early monsoon.

Amaresh Patnaik
THE INNER CHORD

Thousand Suns
The game alters
From moment to moment
A dreamless dawn
Breaks at sunup.

Vibrations
Have the tears gotten any
connect with joy or pain?
The flood sweeps away homes
That builds a naked world
Gain or loss
Transient, immortal
Or transcendental
Life exists therefore.

The Swan
Days, months and years
Laughter with dapples of dreams
Courage-emanating clay
Slowly, the sky gets
Familiar with.

Manorama Biswal Mahapatra
THE RENTED HOUSE

The fragrance
of *korei* and *mahula* flowers
was my childhood.
the voice of the dark bamboo trees
the throb of *kanishiri* leaves.

The house that baked cakes
was my home
the turmeric plants that created a flutter
was my love
How can I feel them in a rented house?
How can I feel the excitement
when we searched for the mouse burrows
to throw the broken canine teeth?

The evening that descended
among the *jahni* blossoms
Patches of dark clouds sailing
over the low clay houses
their thatch-roofs adorned with
pumpkin and *jahni* flowers
They are all the unforgettable moments
of my childhood days.

Today
Am I not the same flickering *jahni* flowers?
their bright essence?
I have buried all my loneliness
under this rented house
leaving aside all the love-soaked calls
of my childhood
How am I engrossed with myself
in the false aristocracy
of this rented house?

Soubhagyabant Maharana
THE BROKEN MIRROR

Often, I have looked at
My own reflection in the mirror
In search life's essence
Under a blind tradition,
Forgetting the place, time and people
Ignoring everything good or bad.

How many times
And in the name of reforms
Should I sharpen the moments
Of joy and grief
Of the past or those of the future?

Caught in the net of life's riddles
I do not know whether
I can be described as
a caballer or a rebel
The entire village folk have gathered
Under the banyan tree to understand this.
But it was too late before
I could grasp the grief
Of the broken looking glass.

All of a sudden I stumble into
The banyan tree's aerial roots
Which have gone deep into the soil
Walking in the dull darkness.

It is at a time
When the blood of the foot
Flows into the muck
And the search for my self continues
In every splinter of the broken glass.

The broken mirror makes me restless
To chase the truth that lies between
Culture and anti-culture
To pen a pleasant or unpleasant foreword
About things-- ominous and non-ominous.
■

Bhagaban Jayasingh
JUST A FEW MOMENTS BEFORE THE HANGING

After sometime
A cruel sound will push me far
Far from the venom of commotion of this world
very far.

I shall drift away
like the mad, turbulent stream
of a river in spate
pushing behind me
many a confusion of
many familiar villages and cities.

After a while
the candlelight will be put out
in the yet-to-blow wind
Darkness will come pushing in
like a sharp, bloody knife.

A sudden and certain terror
will blend in the air
The tears of empathy and anxiety
will dissolve on the face.

A fearful wind
will whip against the trees
The blood will clot in the heart
after a deadly snake bite.

The trust of my friends and
relatives will melt away-
No longer shall the lotus bloom
in the rainwater of their assurances.

The milk from my wife's nipples
will dry up on its own
The uncertain future of my children
will hang on the sharp edge of a sword.

Just a few moments after this
A dark storm will push me
Far, very far
And what can make the earth, the womb of violence,
tremble for some unknown peace!!!
■

Aparna Mohanty
ON MYSELF

You saw
and enjoyed my body
so long.

When touched,
the eyes
like the touch-me-not
folded inward
The breasts
unfolded like a full-bloomed lotus.

In coitus, thrilled
my thighs and youthfulness
were roused.

You enjoyed me
as a bride or a whore
in clothes or without clothes
in artistry or in classic fashion.

When in your eyes
my nakedness turned into an artfulness
It was a taboo to look at myself
for it was ugly, indecent,
a social evil.

After so long
I could see myself
electrified.
I could see
how in the waves of my virgin body
swam a woman's primeval mind
who was denied playfulness so long.

Now who refuses to split into
mother, sister or wife,
goddess or hero.
Look how I build my elegant body
and soul with poetic traits
my new sexual desires!

Forgive me
if I did not look
chaste and pretty
in the mirror of your ego;
Forgive me
if today my eyes discover me
as the prettiest woman on earth
who lives only for love

And the aim of such a love
is nectar, only nectar,
a creation eternal.

Aswini Kumar Mishra
MAELSTROM

Barefoot, they stride along
the road in saffron-flushed attire
with water-pots heavy
on their shoulders to perform
Jalavisek on Jatia Baba's head
for liberating their daughters
from the astral blights of Mars
for shoving Saturn out of
the eighth house from their natal chart.

Riding the wheel of their destiny,
and exhilarated, they drift across
the stream of devotion crossing
many mileposts in their journey
through many villages and cities
without food or sleep
in excruciating pain.

Chanting Bol bum* to
the rhythm of undying rain
pattering down the streets
they move in rapid strides
lest they should miss their Monday rites

lest their flaming consciousness
get extinguished midway
before fulfilment of their quest.

All through the journey
their loud songs of Shiva
like the bright fury of the firecrackers
scare away the minor gods and goddesses
for they fear of being dispossessed
of their places in heaven
and on earth in temples.

Maybe they could rub out differences
between classes
between space and time,
could help Sukru, Mandia and Tikrajani,
don three pairs of attires in saffron,
hold *kamandalu* in hand,
in exchange of axe
that could save Ram Bisei from death.

Perplexed, maybe, Gopi Babu**
should be happy in heaven
there was at least someone
who could touch the Paraja at last.

■

*Bol bum devotees are the followers of Hindu God Shiva called Shaivites. They are mostly seen moving in serpentine queues to different Shiva temples in the month of Shravan. Known as "kanwarias," they undertake hard and arduous journey to offer holy water to their lord. The ritual is seen as fulfilment of their secret vows to God.

** Gopi Babu (Gopinath Mohanty) is the most well-known novelist of Odisha who had won Jnanpith, the highest literary award of India. The character of Ram Bisei, referred to in the poem, is culled from his most admired work Paraja.

Haraprasad Parichha Pattanaik
THE HORIZON

I had to tell a story
To Time that was roaming around,
Explain two lines of truth to memory,
Warn the sea against
moonlight's insolence
which is even unbearable to God.

Now at sundown
A bird has gone wild in the sky
A blooming silence
Begins to paint the chronicles of past life.

Darkness is the antagonist
To the species of birds
which this bird could not understand
Shall never understand too
It might understand its own helplessness
When time will break a twig
On a cup of tea
Though this dark will not.

The sky belongs to no one
Who will explain this and to whom!

The things which appeared to be one's own
Maybe they will be here
Yet wind will not be near him.

Am I born to fork out my life
Chasing after illusion?

Like the wild grass on the river bank
Like a Rangoon-returned Indra, the old man
Like a gold necklace
stacked inside a glass box
Like the meditating past
in the Khandagiri cave
I have always been alone, lifelong.

The horizon, like the sky
is an obscure poem.
Like the whim of the roaming time
Trying to touch the horizon
Of the bird, or else the poet's.

My patience has snapped
So also my time
To explain to others, even to myself
On the earth and beyond the earth
I feel as though the road of illusion
Comes to an end.

I had to call time to tell a story.
■

Hrushikesh Mallick
DIARY OF A BETEL LEAF GROWER

They are not ours, my boys
they are "They"
The devil in the night of the new-moon,
and in the distant grooves
learns from them
how to scare away lonely man
They are night's illusions
of the uprooted days.

Like betel leaf
they hardly understand why
the stomach aches;
betel vine feels morose
yet they do not when
the waist bends under the weight of debt;
insensitive as they are
they do not understand
the pain of indentured labor spreading
through their bone marrows.

Who are they?
nothing except a string of 'commands'
that the red tape entails;

their sweet soft words
cut like a sharp blade;
they have forsaken their childhood
at the village border
and there's no use in making them
understand:
how heaven comes flowing
in a drop of sweat
how a lifelong failure
drains out in a drop of tear.

Leave them alone, my boys
let them raze the pinnacles of our labor pull
down our vineyard
they can hardly understand
what the protest is
they have been asked to turn to
a stone till the work is done…
Stretch out your hands
let them place a shackle round your wrists
let them remain young forever
a flock of sheep.

Let us go back to our huts, boys,
and holding each other's hand
cry although the night
Grandpa used to say:
God takes birth in tears
You might not have heard it, my boys
but I have.

Pravasini Mahakud
THE BOUNTIFUL

Driven by the importunate need of a star
She had flung open her window
when she saw a handful of stars
hanging from a *gangasiuli* plant.

As she badly pined for a flower
One day she opened her door
to see thousands of lotus flowers
which had bloomed in the nearby pond.

She had to enter into a dialogue
with a bird when she saw
thousands of blue and white birds
flying from sea to sea.

One day she turned back
to see the past
But before she could glance through it
She had transformed herself into the past.

In anticipation of some news
One morning she realized that
she had changed into a piece of news
and hogged the headlines herself.

Once she wanted a lump of clouds
But she could not know
When she had burst into rain
To flow on earth.

Once she wanted burst into flame
But she saw how
The flame-of-the-forest
and goldmohur have lighted
a torch everywhere.

Looking at the wailing earth
under the cover of darkness
She thought to herself how to
Come out of her own self
But could she manage to accomplish it?

The star, lotus, bird, the past
news, clouds and torch
all had surrounded her on all sides

Later it was known how
She has metamorphosed into
history in the rock inscriptions
and on the stone walls of the temples.
∎

Shatrughna Pandab
A TALE OF A PHALANX

There is a phalanx everywhere.

The true hero knows
How to fight
While fighting he kills
Or, is killed
This is his destiny, he knows.

Whose memorial is it
That has wiped out his name
Whose name is it
That the forehead of time sparkles?

Nonchalantly
It stares into the future
That buoys up a warrior
Who marches ahead
To the sound of trumpets
And meets the seven great warriors

Face to face
Alone.

Amarendra Khatua

PASSAGE OF LIFE

A deep dark night:
The coal back moonless shadows
pervade
beyond the eyes could see.

Like death.

A quiet and lifeless body
dependable no more
sprouts on a heap of dead petals
like silence hovering over
tree stems.

Thus the time passes waiting
in dread
without precepts.

It seems as though
in every night's last breath
the breath of the light
will spread sunlight on the trees
to quench the thirst of
the dew-filled grass.

Flowers will bloom again.
And my absence will
stir a life
in the unknown roadside trees.

Prasanna Kumar Mohanty
SORROWS ARE NOT AT FAULT

Forgive the sorrows.

How can they live
Without the graceful benevolence
Of each one of you?

They have mastered
A prehistoric art
Like the terrorists
who fire from their automatic rifles
From their hiding;
It's their eternal instinct
To open the sluice gates of
A reservoir without
Warning;
It's their family trade
To tear down the conch-white pinnacles
Of your joy;
And crush the half-formed words
Of an unfashioned poem
With their terrifying cruelty.

Don't blame it on them.

They live on the evanescing age
Of your happiness
Like mosquitos;
They feast on the blood
Of your good fortune;
They breathe the poison of
Deadly serpents
Their soul thrives on
The angry clashes of a heartless sword.

Forgive them for this life only.
■

Binapani Panda
THE WAR

The war wages throughout the night,
In darkness
Or in a chunk of dim light
that had fallen on the bed's edge.
In the eye's silent revolt
Or in the lips' select words.

The closed door, the open casement,
The sky, the stars, the moon
The rain, darkness and wind
All are the participants in the war
Either on the side of foes
Or of friends.

The war has not just begun
It has been raging for ages
Since I have started to
recognize call of the eyes
Hunger of the body
Their rights since my birth.

Since I knew the difference between
Light and darkness
Unraveled mystery why flowers bloom
Played the game of fire to burn
Or make others burn;
The heart weak as wet clay
Has turned into a war field
Yet I have used my hand as armor
Wrapped my consciousness
with the shield of indifference
Equipped my forehead with a helmet
Yet, I am not free from the pain of war.

Is there any certain principle of war?
Why is a deadly hatred yearned for
In war and love?
A deluge sets in just over the night
That sweeps away both heaven and hell
Morning announces a complete ceasefire
All the unwritten accords
Appear as fingermarks in water.

Pitambar Tarai

A PATCH OF LAND

It took one and a half years to come to hand.

What trouble have I not faced
all these days:
There was not a day that
I have not drenched
the frost, the dew and the sun,
my sense of incompetence
my half-baked intellect.

Brother, whatever you might say
All sorrows are but the indistinct breaths
of a tall palm,
Within me lies
a screw pine forest of unexpressed sighs
How dear they are to me!

Now I could realize
river's relationship with thirst
Why life feels like a bubble
It is for this only I was searching
for a patch of land.

If the dripping age is gone
like the bullocks. Let it.
I could at least acquire
a four *gunth* patch of land
which my ancestors could not.

Now the wall will rise, the house will stand
on its own, one house only.

Hereafter my father's name,
the name of my village, clan
all will spruce up my being
like the thatch of a house
like the creeping pumpkin tendrils
of my hope and hopelessness
My destiny will shine like a moonlit night.

Coitus in one room,
A blabbermouth, my son cannot sleep
dreaming of a throne
My daughter will spend sleepless nights
writing letters to her lover
Leave me alone,
I must get ready to pack up
or, hang like an uncalled-for skeleton
from a chair.

I never thought I had to ponder so much
and realize how one had to
burn oneself for ages to acquire
a patch of land
I now understand why my ancestors
could not procure a patch of land for so long! ∎

Senapati Pradyumna Keshari
CREMATION GROUND

Why fear the burial ground?
It's safer than home, cozier than bed
Warmer than mother's saree's edge
Deeper than the river's hot caress.

What's the sun? What's the rain?
Or autumn's dew-laden cool silence?
It always murmurs a mellifluous tune.

While playing fire and ash
the rain bugs of sweet separation
crawl on the field of his eyes
her furtive glances hiding
the lazy and unforgettable coos
of a heart fraught with honey.

As the house that looks pretty
embellished with love and devotion
the cremation ground looks unique
adorned with dialogues
of solitude and silence.

Like a newly married young woman
when her husband goes abroad
the cremation ground
feels the pinch of bereavement
through the rising curls of smoke.

The cremation ground, a place
that reverberates with
an unbroken chain of events
like a temple it never closes its door,
but remains busy in mehfils.

The cremation ground is a friend
whom everybody loves to meet
its familiarity no one ever detests
maybe it never bursts into tears
yet, its unshed tears are
more tender than a flower.
■

Pradeep Biswal

AN EVENING AT CHANDIPUR-ON-SEA

The silent sea is asleep
like the sick time
or the kittenish sea crabs;
sometimes the reluctant wind
indicates its own unwellness.

Desolate look
the casuarina trees on the beach
like the tired questions
in the bleak moonlight
when someone calls me by name
is he a relative of my own who is no more
or my successor
who is yet to arrive on the stage.

If there is no one here around
solitude turns hollow
one has to search for
his own existence
in the ever-stretching
shore of time.

Sometimes I feel
I am the past myself
I am also the future myself
like the waves retreating after
striking against the shore.

I continued to ask these little crabs
what's the color of blood
blue or red?
they slip into their sand burrows
without any idea about
my relationship with them.

After I came back to
the solitary *dak* bungalow
the waves of questions
blast me like the agitated sea
I bid adieu to the beach
in the silent, solitary night.

Surya Mishra

WORDS

Words descend with multiple luck.

Pure, sinless, sweet and indelible,
they love to accompany creation
which one can conserve for life;
they fill the body
with sweet, scintillating thrill of love
We also think of them as gods,
Pay our obeisance to them
They are the manifestation of
Satya, Shiva and *Sundar.*

Absurd and false looks their life
like the leaves as they fall under the tree
on an evening earth
they float, dry up, wilt;
and trampled under feet they turn into powder,
they stink, become a part of the soil,
rise up to the dust-infested sky,
become weak under the impact of wind;
shattered they run helter shelter
they get lost in memory.

Shorn off their courage
they look like the cemetery of dreams
corpse of hope
inauspicious dreams of a dark night
the curse of a ghost.

Burnt up in bright sunlight
shedding tears
blinded in an accident
the words are chosen after much thoughts
good or bad
saint or devil
innocent or wicked
pretty or ugly
pure or polluted.

Sometimes the words burn in heart
like a wick
and get lost in the embrace
of a silent death.

Kamal Kumar Mohanty
SINS

Sins can be woven together
Like a chaplet of flowers
That could hang
From the neck of darkness.

The earth is pregnant with sins
Yet, I have never complained before
The sky, the fire or the water
With a belief
That one day all the sins
would exhaust themselves
On their own at daybreak.

Who would then
Let the night break into day?
The flower-studded music of desire
The fresh blossoms of hope
As they wilt without reason.

Darkness unfold its plans
Like a film showing a streak of tigers
Chasing a frightened deer
When disrobed, the earth shudders
As the naked eyes look at her,
Or, when some others try to capture
Her nakedness on their camera lens.

The earth stands as a mute witness
To their act of fleecing her
Without a wisp of a protest.

Darkness
As it strengthens its foundation
Sins continue to string together
Their new experience of rot.

Ajay Pradhan
THE CLAN

The girl whom the courtiers raped
repeatedly
when the court was in session
is my sister.
The news of the accused
roaming free comes thick and fast
police can do nothing,
they have absconded since long.

The person who has died
without a morsel of rice
while laying road or a building or factory
is my Pa
whose pyre I lit made me see lines of black
and got twenty-seven rupees
as compensation.

The utility and the wall
if they look sparkling clean
she is my Maa
who keeps the newborn warm
and its feces clean
An epileptic, she has not enough blood,
says the doctor.

My only brother who went to the city
to work for an executive
The landlady lodged a police complaint
with her daughter as a witness
Then no one knows how
he was found dead run over
by a truck.

The boy who sweeps crumbs
at a hotel is my brother
The woman who uses a shovel
to mix cement with chips
is my wife
We are all workaholics, we
do not aspire to be free
for all of us work is god, day and night.

What is really happening
Is there anything that is unknown to
you, my Lord!
∎

Satya Pattanaik
THE IMMIGRANT

Do not please think
I have wiped out footprints
from my homeland.

The land I have stepped into
has turned into gold
The oyster I have touched
has transformed into pearl.

New York's
Manhattan Stock Exchange
has stood on my sinewy legs
All the technological experiments
at Redmond in Washington
are only the expressions
of my own vision
Immigrant transmits knowledge
but never bends his head.

All your discoveries and inventions
bear the stamp of my hand
The immigrant grows
green grapes in the Napa Valley
mandarins in Florida
with no grouse.
His own sweat
has filled your wine and fruit juice bottles
You have sung the incoherent ghazals
of your conquest with
the unexpressed sighs of his heart.

Remember
when paddy becomes ripe
The season of harvest sets in
Invocation song rings in his ears
The immigrant comes back
to the lap of his soil.
∎

Rakshak Nayak
THE BLACKBOX

The flight was fabulous.

After being separated from you
my body began to shake
mysterious and thrilling
was the upward journey
Death only patted my back
to wish me a long life.

Gruesome was this flight,
extension of an enticement,
a sculpture of time
When down below
the artillery like cannon and mortar
lay in readiness.

We did not have any destination to hit.
Our only aim was to fly
to savor freedom's fragrance
when like old memories
the landscape began to blur
when like a dot
the hills, forests and hamlets
all moved in unison on the plains.

Up above the clouds
the planets, stars and starlets
all came flying nearer
indicating a heaven
not very far.

The people on earth
glowed like glowworms
Have they forgotten about us?

Suddenly a technical snag
and fire encircling the plane
put us in the throes of death
The cockpit looked empty
The pilots had melted into thin air
Now, we had to turn into ash
that we had abandoned
looking skyward.

How soon has the hemlock of love
has emptied itself
Our end was not natural
but an accident of some sort
Who can give us an answer
who's responsible for the crash?

Down below
not just we, but everyone else
shall wait for the black box
Aha!
■

Sunil Kumar Prusty
A PRAYER FOR MY SON

Come, I will wrap you
with the warmth of my sorrowful sigh.

My sorrow and sigh are my own,
Personal.

No one should scribble a father's
karma on the destiny of his son
Let him be a God.
In his childhood. In his dreams.
Remember my son
I'm your drunkard Paa
The tear and repentance
of a drunken spring.

Hiding from your Maa
I gleaned the golden corns
from a love-laced field
on the banks of the river Mahanadi
a slice of poetry on the bird's beak.
Nothing could I give you
I have also forgotten the song
I wrote.

Don't ever my son ignore me
I'm innocent like a splendid line of a poem
Are you not magnificent line
Of a superb poem?

If each father becomes a poet
Should not he ask for
a Godlike son's compassion?
If each father becomes a poet
Does not he give in to
the pressure domestic chores?

My loving son
You are a poet of your little feet
I am not. Not at all.
∎

Sucheta Mishra

THE WHORE

It's a boat
that has snapped its ties
It has lost its oars…

A boat that has no boatswain
The wild waves only
Fling themselves into the sky
Hold them tight to fling again.

How should
A naked helplessness
Of a body turn into
An ultimate barbaric insult?

The fresh leaf the tree has shed
Rots in the mud
Someone calls her by name
The moon has not graced the sky as yet.

Scared of police and the AIDS
The morning has tiptoed away
It has not come back again.
Dreams continue to hang
From the customers' apparels
On the cot's edge.

The worm that wipes out the clutter
Thrives on the clutter alone
Forgetting its own response
Which you call life.

The bedspread is all stains
And stains only
Can any pricey soap blot them out?
■

Amiya Ranjan Mohapatra
THE ADULTEROUS HAND OF LIGHT

Do I look like myself
after I turned into a stone?

What do I have now my own
like the past that had decked
my foot and palm with lotus flowers
a heart with lotus buds
and the body with lotus petals?

Like in the past
Can you taste on my lips
the bright darkness of *asadha*
anymore or, the onset of untimely rains
in the passing winds of my naked plaits?

Do the butterflies and bees
encircle me as before,
Do I sit here alone
under the new cloak of my loneliness,
Do my eyes close
when the light of debauchery
touches me as before?

Do I still wear
the saree and glass bangles
after I have turned into a stone?
Still I lie here naked and shameless!

Have not I been stripped off
the lotus pond,
the moonlight of the hills
and mind's hunger?
Have not the sunlight forgotten to see
his face in a dew drop?

I do not know how a piece of stone
carols with glee to feel
the warmth of *phalgun*,
Does the light of the moon
flow from the heart of autumn?
Or, my champak finger
strum a violin in the *asadha* wind?

Am I a guest, a stranger in my own body?
A futile preparation
for my next birth?

I cannot free myself from
the womb of stone
as if my soul were brimming with
indolence for ages.
I do not know how long
should my defeated past
follow me like this?

Suresh Nayak
THE PROTAGONIST

I have come back, Mr. Spectator
A hero I am, I stand here
on top of my grandmother's tale.

Yesterday, the man who
was shot dead by a terrorist,
the martyr, whose body
you carried on your shoulder to
the burning *ghat* was me.
Where is my death? I am deathless.

Today, the tale is different.
The roleplay is different.

I am the one
who has dismantled the hives of wasps
helped the honey to ooze out
of the mountain top.

The hand that dropped food grains
from the sky
for those who lived encircled by
flood water was mine.

The struggle of the landless
does not need a gun, Comrade!
Why not hurl a bomb?

Come, I shall teach you the technique
how to bring out flowers and fruits
with the hand of the raw soil
and your feet with
the hooves of the black horses
The road will stretch for miles.

Your hunger does not need
the blood of yet another hungry, my Friend
Come over the stage
of myriad hopes
for the ultimate spectacle.
■

K. Shyamababu Dora
ONCE AGAIN

Let me strum a note for the last time
Lest it should be too late
And agonies should die down.

Many a time have I metamorphosed
Myself into a tree and woodcutter.
Each time that as a tree I've embellished myself with
flowers, fruits and leaves
I've sharpened myself with new hopes
And assurances.

Now I have to turn to nothing
Neither to a tree
Nor to a woodcutter,
But transform myself to a few lines of verse
And all for the last time.

Now I've to coax a flower
The flower that is me
A boat has to sink midstream
The boat that is me.

Now I've put my head
On the altar of sacrifice
To share my blood, flesh and bones
Among the impoverished lot.
I wish to be born among them
As part of the crowd of the hungry.
∎

Swapna Mishra
HISTORY

Beyond a half-broken wall
Lies buried
A history of many a victory and defeats
The story of a soul that is wounded and dead.

On this side flows a river
Its water reflects a face
Magnificent as the moon.

Many a time it calls me
Winking in silence
It goes on telling its story
Whether I hear or not.

So much of water has flown away
In the river
Yet the path of its stream
remains untraced
So many voices have lost
On its breast
They seem to be endless.

I can hear everything
Yet history stands a guard
Against my moving ahead
Does history have a sutra to life?

I can hear the jingle of anklets
Which comes ringing from its *ranga mahal*
The peals of laughter
The sound of horse hooves
Their incessant neighs
The curls of smoke filling the sky
The blood stains on the battle ground.

I don't know how a tremulous hand
Stretches forward
At times its palm gets wet with a drop of tear
Or a patch of clouds.
■

Sharmistha Sahoo
DEAR BUTCHER

My dear Butcher
Your lethal blade shines hundred suns.

After a frantic search for a hiding place
I have trespassed into you
I am now scared
that your copper complexion
might overpower my soft limbs.

Maybe like horizon
you are an illusion,
and walking on earth and an easy prey
I am almost extinct like a bird.

When I looked around to see the sky
It was you
When I looked around for the earth
It was you.

Free from the tether
My closed palm had mantric rice and flowers
The sacrificial altar looked
so very exciting!

O my dear Killer
I do not want the language of my blood
should quieten you
The wild wind of self-slaughter
blow through your long fingers.

I never wanted the sun to turn blue
Blood of the moon or star to flow from the sky.

The silence that echoed the jingle of bangles
might turn silent
The wick that burned in my blood
might be put out
on the hazardous street of your glance.

Before the jungle is set on fire
rocks suck away all the water
Remove the flower garland
from around my neck
Let me go back,

whether with or no verve
but surely in body on the road of my own.
■

Kedar Mishra

THE WESTERN STATE

Dreaming of flower
Or of white elephants
The women of western state
Who are black
As night of the new moon,

The farmer's blood
Turns into water, every year,
Every season the forest's knotted vein
Gets uprooted
The silver stream loses its sheen
Drying up midway.

The family head has his home
His own village,
Yet, he lives abroad
He has his field but there is none to till
The bunch of soot black clouds
Float away.

Chaitra sets in
Spreading across Dhulia's farmyard
The juice oozes out drop by drop
The flowers bloom
Round the season.

The dark countryside
Burns churning in the dark
The man of the western state.

All the west has no sun
Light is forbidden to enter
Now a message has come
That a man of the western state
Has fashioned the morning
into a weapon.
■

Manoj Kumar Meher
THE BIRD

That day we divided our mother
When Chhotu, my younger brother agreed
to give seven months of aliments
and I for five months.

If the slave of the sun or rain
devastates the bird's nest
If the silent ladylove of winter
scatters away the morning that is dead
Aha!
The bird strums a tune of kinship
With tears crushed within
It has never robbed anyone's artistry
It has never usurped anyone's joy
It has never dumped the burning embers
on a happy home
With a mind as high as the sky
it flew through the deep hell of the soul.

No, no bloodshed for Mother
No, no knife wounds for wealth
Aha!
Being separated from the loved one
the bird continues to sob in sorrow.

That day, as we lit father's pyre
Chhotu took
all the irrigated land
and I, the open land adjacent to our home
Thus we divided our mother that day.
■

Bijayalaxmi Parida
RED HIBISCUS

It had to bloom yesterday
But it did not.
The forehead of goddess for whom
Advance was paid
Remained bare

Why does it brag about
A chunk of clay, a pinch of the sky
And a frail branch?
It had slept among the foliage
It did not answer to my repeated queries
As to what made her cry
Last night.

It's simple 'yes' would have made
The temple pigeons fly
To the other side and come back
With *Kaluribent's* two magic wands
Even though a little too late.

Yet, it did not know
How to share its joys, never
Now it would get up, wash its face,
Wipe it clean, put a red *bindi*
And laugh away the day, doting…
Maybe stumbling a little.

Now it would sink to bed
And never tell, even though
One asks him repeatedly
As to why it bursts into tears
Every night.
■

Gayatribala Panda
INSECT

How easy it is to spring
into fire!

This is how death lures
one into oblivion.

It is not the time to blame it on luck
Fire licks away everything around
Wind wafts in the burn out smell
everywhere.

No one looks cold with fear
Neither the time nor the god
The story of a wrong-doing done
sometimes back
The tale of someone melting into the void
free from indebtedness to earth.

See, how glamorous looks fire's deceit
which can transform
the ancient disquiet into moments of silence
turn life into ash, just in moments.

The blind cannot see the fire, insects, death
The distance between
one platform and the other
shape of the earth like
a one-rupee coin or of a lemon?

The insect cannot see the flame and death
All that it can see is its mad desire
to take a leap into its own swinishness.

What more is life?
It is like a fish bone that gets stuck
in the throat, emitting a woeful sigh
at times unknown.
■

CONTRIBUTORS

Sachi Routray (1916-2004). Sachidananda, popularly known as Sachi Routray, has been hailed as the inaugurator of a new age in Odia poetry. His fame as a poet of new trends and sensibility rests on the publication of *Pandulipi* (1947) and *Kabita 1962* (1962), which helped him break away from the cramping romantic tradition of Odia poetry, initiated by the Sabuja poets. He became a household name in Odisha after the publication of *Pallishree* and *Baji Rout*. He had a career that spanned over more than fifty years as a poet, essayist, literary critic, story writer and novelist. His collections include *Patheya, Bhanumatira Desh* (poetry), *Chitragrib* (novel), *Mashanira Phul* (short story). He received the Jnanapith, India's highest literary award, apart from the Soviet Land Nehru award and Sahitya Akademi award. Government of India conferred on him Padmashri, country's fourth highest civilian award for his overall contribution to art and literature.

Binod Chandra Nayak (1919-2003). His collections of poems include *Haimanti, Nila Chandrar Upatyaka, Sata Tarar Dwip, Ilabrutta, Sarisrup* and *Pohala Dwipar Upakatha*. He began his career as a Lecturer in Odia and retired as Principal of a non-government college of the state. He was awarded by Central Sahitya Akademi for his book *Sarisrup* (1970).

Guruprasad Mohanty (1924-2004) is arguably the most influential Odia poet of 1950s. He had written only sixty eight poems, including ten sonnets during his lifetime which are scattered in only three exiguous volumes of poetry: *Nutan Kabita, Samudra Snan* and *Ascharya Abhisar*. Guruprasad's sonnets became extremely popular among his readers. He received Sahitya Akademi award (1973) for *Samudra Snana*. He was the Principal of a local degree college in his hometown of Bhubaneswar before his retirement and death.

Bhanuji Rao (1926-2001). His first book of poems *Nutan Kabita* was written in collaboration with his poet friend Guruprasad Mohanty. Some of his most appreciated works of poetry include *Bishad Ek Ruutu, Nai Arapari, Chandan Banare Eka* and *Shabda Sange Shringar*. He received Sahitya Academy award in 1989 for *Nai Arapari*. He was an instructor at Lal Bahadur Shastri Academy of Administration for a long time before retirement.

Chintamani Behera (1927-2005). After getting a degree in Odia language and literature from Calcutta University, Chintamani worked in various government colleges. He also served as Secretary of Odisha Sahitya Akademi. His most important poetical works include *Swetapadma, Hey Vaidehi Bhulija, Trutiya Chakshu* and *Nije Nijar Sathi*. He won the Sahitya Akademi award.

Rabi Singh (b.1930) Rabi Singh sought to inspire people through his writings, advocating equality among all humans which remained at the center of his creation from the beginning. He attacked social injustice and backwardness in society in all his poems collected in volumes including *Patha Prantar Kabita, Charam Patra* and *Anaryar Charyapad*. He bagged the state Sahitya Akademi award for his book *Charamapatra*. He also won the Atibadi Jagannath Das Samman, the highest literary honor (2017).

Uma Shankar Panda (1931-2015). Though Umashankar's poetic style did not change greatly over his lifetime, his initial lyrical wonder continued to attract the readers till the end. Some of his well-received poetical works are: *Romantic Kabita, Iman Kalyan, Nishabda Nupur, Kalar Bhumistha Shabda* and *Rati Rati Ruutuparna*. He won the Sahitya Akademi award.

Ramakanta Rath (b.1934). A former member of the Indian Administrative Service, Ramakanta has been acclaimed as a very powerful poet, who has influenced a whole generation of young poets after him. His early volumes of poetry like *Anek Kothari* and *Sandgdha Mrugaya* have been considered as ushering in a new kind of poetry in the expression of a new taste and sensibility of the age. His later collection of poetry *Sri Radha* became extremely popular with readers and critics alike. Ramakanta has been the recipient of the "Saraswati Samman" and "Sahitya Academy Fellowship." He was conferred with "Padma Bhushan", country's third highest civilian award for his distinguished service in the field of literature. His collections of poetryinclude *Kete Dinar, Anek Kothari, Saptam Rutu, Sachitra Andhar, Sri Palatak* and *Simantabas*.

Sarat Chandra Pradhan (b.1934). His published poetry collections include *Hansa O Saras, Uchaishraba, Yajati* and *Batrish Sinhasan*. He has since retired as Professor of Odia from the Sambalpur University.

Brahmotri Mohanty (1934-2010). She received widespread popularity among the common readers, after the publication of her book *Drusti O Dyuti*. Her honors include a state Sahitya Akademi award for *Drusti O Dyuti*. Her later poetry centered round her spiritual experience inherent in her poetry collection, *Srotaswati*.

Kamalakant Lenka (1934-1999). Many of Kamalakant's best-known poems are about the people, their existential angst, their loneliness, insanity, and death. His published books of poems include *Preeti O Pratiti, Uttaran, Kabitar Munha, Nija Saha Gote Sakshatakar Khasibar Bel* and *Gita Gaanare Pakshi*. A winner of the state Sahitya Akademi award, Kamalakant was a Reader in Odia serving in different government colleges of the state.

Bibek Jena (1935-1985). Bibek is best remembered for his poetry collection, *Pabanar Ghar* published in 1971. His other collections are *Devi, Smruti,* and *Kimbadanti*.

Jagannath Prasad Das (b.1936). He did his Masters from the University of Allahabad and after a short teaching career there joined the Indian Administrative Service but left it to devote himself to full time writing and research. He has published eleven volumes of poetry, eight collections of short stories, a novel, two collections of essays and five plays besides a number of books of children's verses. A Ph.D. in Art History, he has to his credit several books on Odishan Art. His works have been widely translated into English, Hindi and other Indian languages and his plays have been staged in many languages all over India. He is a recipient of the Sahitya Akademi Award, the Saraswati Samman and the Nandikar Theatre Award. Some of his very well-known books of poetry are: *Pratham Purush, Anya Sabu Mrutyu, Je Jahara Nirjanata, Anhika, Anyadesh Bhinna Samay, Sthir Chitra* and *Smrutir Sahar*. Besides, *Desh Kala Patra* is considered his magnum opus.

Bibhudatta Mishra (1936-2003). An extremely popular poet of the 1960's, Bibhudatta drew the readers' attention for his treatment of love and romance. His *Urbashir Chithi*, published in 1961 was a heartthrob of the young readers. He taught Odia literature in various government colleges.

Brajanath Rath (1936-2014). A progressive poet of eminence, his poetry anthologies include *Maru Golap, Nijaswa Sanlap, Manar Manachitra* and *Hey Mahajivan*. He was awarded the Justice Harihar Mahapatra Memorial award.

Sitakant Mahapatra (b.1937). Winner of the state and central Sahitya Akademi awards, besides India's highest literary honor "Jnanapith," Sitakant is a major voice of the contemporary Indian poetry. A well-known civil servant, critical writer and social anthropologist, he has published over twenty five volumes of poetry including *Astapadi, Samudra, Samayar Shesh Nam* and *Pheri Asibar Bela*. His poetry and critical works have received immense critical attention from inside India and abroad. The President of India conferred on him the Padma Bhushan and Padma Vibhushan in recognition of his outstanding contribution to literature.

Deepak Mishra (1937-2008). A former President of Odisha Sahitya Akademi, Deepak has published over ten volumes of poetry to his credit. *Asamipika, Anustup, Nisidha*

Hrada, Madhyanhar Chhai, Saptam Pruthibi, Arana Mainishi and *Ruuk* are some of his well-known collections of poetry. He won both state and central Sahitya Akademi awards.

Sourindra Barik (1938-2016). Well- known for his "Cycle" poems, Sourindra is also a critic of eminence. Some of his significant collections of poetry include *Samanya Kathan, Upabharat, Akash Pari Nibida* and *Sabuthare Tame*. He won both the state and central Sahitya Akademi awards.

Soubhagya Kumar Misra (b.1940). Soubhagya has published several volumes of poetry, including *Atmanepadi, Madhyapadalopi, Nai Panhara, Andha Mahumachhi, Dwa Suparna, Charachar* and *Matrasparsha*. His honors include both the state and central Sahitya Akademi awards and Iowa Honorary Fellowship. He is a retired Professor of English of Berhampur University.

Nityanand Pati (1940-1989). Nityanand was a prolific writer. His published collections include *Nabikar Nishwas, Nisarta Nilaya, Mouna Muharta, Chhai Aslesha*.

Nityanand Nayak (b.1940). Nityanand has retired as Reader in English. His poetry collections include *Bidirna Maral, Trasta Padmasan, Bhor Sakal* and *Panthasala*. He is also awarded by Sahitya Akademi for poetry.

Banshidhar Sarangi (b.1940) A state and central Sahitya Akademi awardee, Banshidhar has authored several anthologies of poetry in Odia, Hindi and English. His poetic journey has started with the publication of *Samay Asamaya*, followed by *Sthabir Aswarohi* and *Shabaricharya* which received Odisha state Sahitya Akademi award for 1991. Some of his other collections include *Chhayadarshan, Suryoday*. Banshidhar has retired as a Principal.

Harihar Mishra (b.1941). A poet, critic, short story writer and playwright, Harihar is the recipient of a number of literary awards, including the Sarala award. He has published several collections including *Shankhanabhi, Aksham Devata, Chahani Mandap* and *Sandhya Darshan*. He is one of the pioneering poets of the Anam Movement of Odia poetry. Recently Odisha Sahitya Akademi has published *Divine Discontent*, a translation of his book *Dibya Asantosh* from Odia.

Prasanna Kumar Mishra (1941-2014). Prasanna is a poet who is most widely known for his long poem *Truck Dalare Sanatan*. Some of his other books of poetry are *Ratna Dwipar Majhi, Basantar Sketch, Adrushya Sangam, Kharare Bangara Loka*. He is the recipient of several literary awards including Sarala Award and state Sahitya Akademi.

Saroj Ranjan Mohanty (b.1942). Well-known for his romantic love for life and nature, Saroj has been the editor of the prestigious literary journal *Jhankar* for over four decades. His major collections of poetry include *Kagaj Dangar Shoka, Baigeni Rutu* and *Chitramegha*.

Dilip Das (b.1942) Dillip's first book of poems *Bilupta Samrajya* was published in 1980, followed by *Pakshitia Basichhi Dalare Chhai Tar Pokhari Jalare*, a year after, which was an instant success. A recipient of Odisha Sahitya Akademi award his other collections are *Suduraru Anek Dur, Budi Jauthiba Desh, Nilamadhab* and *Batya*.

Pramod Kumar Mohanty (b.1942). His notable works include *Kramahsha, Devipad, Akatakat, Asaranti Anasar, Alagakuha and Chitra Chitrak Chitrapedi*. He is the winner of the Jhankar and Sahitya Akademi awards. He has retired from the Department of Higher Education as Reader in Psychology.

Praharaj Satyanarayan Nanda (b.1943). Satya Narayan was associated with the English daily Amrit Bazar Patrika and Odisha Review as editor. Some of his most significant works of poetry include *Nila Hansar Jwala, Shaba Sangam O Anyanya Kabita, Hiranmeyen Patren* and *Nakshatra Sangam O Anyanya Kabita*.

Niranjan Padhi (b.1943). Niranjan is the author of sixteen collections of poetry, besides four collections of lyrics and one volume of haiku poems. His poetry books *Kalahandir Kavya* and *Samakoir Swapna* are based on Niranja's experience of working as the District Msgistrate in the tribal areas of the state. Some of his other works include *Kafinar Swar, Shunya Nirabata* and very recently published *Chitradhwani*.

Phani Mohanty (b.1944). Essentially romantic by heart, Phani has earned critical acclaim as a poet of love and nature. He is the recipient of state and central Sahitya Akademi awards. His poetry collections include the popular *Priyatama*, a collection of forty four love poems, besides *Manachitra, Swayambar* and *Bishad Joga*. Phani has since retired from the Department of Higher Education as Reader in Philosophy.

Rajendra Kishore Panda (b.1944). A former member of

the Indian Administrative Service, Rajendra has been a very significant voice of the 1970s in Odisha. He has authored over fifteen collections of poetry including *Gouna Devata, Shatadru Anek, Shailakalpa* and *Anya* which are some of his widely read and well appreciated books of poetry. He is the recipient of a string of literary awards including central Sahitya Academy award, the prestigious Gangadhar Meher National Poetry Award, Sachi Rautaray Poetry Award and Bharatiya Bhasha Parishad poetry award.

Nilamani Parida (b.1944). A poet of substance, Nilamani edits *Adhunik*, a literary magazine which marks a half-yearly appearance from Kendrapara. He has authored eight collections of poetry, including *Nadi Nakshatra, Chaturtha Pada* and *Manorama Kahani*.

Haraprasad Das (b.1945). One of the most influential modernist avant-garde writers of Odisha, Haraprasad has handled almost all literary forms including poetry, novels, criticism with utmost dexterity. He has authored more than twenty collections of poetry, including *Mantrapatha, Garbhagruha, Harmoniumare Todi*. He has also received a string of literary awards, including the prestigious Moorti Devi literary award for *Vansha*, state and central Sahitya Academy awards and the Sarala award. A member of the Indian Audits and Accounts Service, he was the Deputy Comptroller General of India before his retirement.

Gopalakrushna Rath (1945-2016). Gopalakrushna has published six poetry collections, including *Ekla Manish, Ketedur, Bipul Digant, Bihwal Belabhumi* and *Arun Udbhas*. He is the recipient of both the state and central Sahitya Academy awards. He started his career as a judge but shifted to academics later, and retired as Professor of Law from Sambalpur University. Then he renounced the material world to live the life of an ascetic till his death.

Nrusingh Prasad Tripathy (b.1945). Nrusingh is the editor of Nabalipi, a prestigious literary quarterly, which has a history of over thirty years of uninterrupted publication. A former Director of Income Tax, he has published around ten books of poetry, including *Hey Ishwar Utha, Parba, Bujhamana, Nidrita Sanyas, Sunya Raman, Pranay Param Ved* and more recently *Thai Nathai*. He refused to receive the Sahitya Akademi award which was conferred on him in 2003.

Prativa Satapathy (b.1945). One of the foremost women poets of Odisha, Prativa shot into eminence in the 1970s with a volume of poems entitled *Asta Jahnar Elegy*. Some of her very well-known poetry anthologies include *Shahada Sundari, Shabari, Tanmay Dhuli* and *Adha Adha Nakshyatra*. She has bagged both the state and central Sahitya Akademi awards. An academic by profession, she edits a poetry magazine, *Udbhas*, after her retirement.

Prasanna Kumar Patasani (b.1946) A four-time Member of Parliament, Patasani had already established himself as a poet of substance before he made his foray into the world of politics. He has published several volumes of poetry, including *Akar Kabita, Bagha Aaanre Picnic, Barsha, Sapa Gatare Sakal, Dekhahele Kahibi Sekatha* and *Akashar Kathagadare Bandi Suryanku Jera*.

Ashutosh Parida (b.1946) shot into eminence with *Chandal*, which received widespread appreciation from the readers soon after its publication. His other poetical works include *Ipsit Krodh, Shabdabhedi, Raktabarnar Bali* and *Angargar*. A Ph.D in Mechanical Engineering, Asutosh has since retired from Regional Research Laboratory, Bhubaneswar as a senior scientist. He has won Bhanuji Rao poetry samman and Odisha Sahitya Akademi award.

Devdas Chhotray (b.1946). A poet, lyricist, composer, screen playwright, Devdas was widely known in the literary circles much before his first collection of poetry *Neel Saraswati* which was published in 1984. He has composed lyrics for more than seventy five films. A former member of the Indian Administrative Service, he had worked in many senior administrative positions before he joined Ravenshaw University as its first Vice Chancellor. Apart from *Neel Saraswati*, Devdas has authored three collections of poetry, *Hati Saj Kar, Nua Luha Puruna Luha* and *Mallika*. He is the recipient of prestigious Bishuba award.

Mamata Dash (b.1947) is a widely published woman poet who has authored nine books of poetry, including *Naimisharanya, Ekatra Chandra Surya* and *Mayandhakar*. Besides, she also writes fiction and criticism. She is the recipient of a flurry of literary awards, including state Sahitya Akademi and Bharatiya Bhasha Parishad poetry awards.

Baikunthanath Sahoo (b.1948). A poet with six anthologies of poems to his credit, Baikunthanath entered the creative world of writing even before he started his career in Odisha Administrative Service. Apart from *Hrudayakunj*, some of his commendable works of poetry include *Satyapath, Samayar Chhabidekha* and *Batabana Nadi*.

Sarojini Sarangi (b.1948). Beginning to write in the early seventies, Sarojini has emerged as an important woman voice today. She has eight collections of poetry to her credit, among which *Ajanma* has been hailed as her magnum opus. The title poem has been done into a documentary film by Padmashri Neelamadhab Panda. By profession a gynecologist, Sarojini also writes on women's health issues.

Amaresh Patnaik (b.1948). Some of his collection of poems are *Manaru Manaku, Sandhi Bisandhi* and *Abudha Garuda.* He has received the state Sahitya Akademi award for poetry and central Sahitya Akademi award for translation. Amaresh was on the editorial board of Soviet Land and *Pratibeshi.* Currently he is on the Odia Advisory Board of Sahitya Akademi, New Delhi.

Manorama 'Biswal' Mahapatra (b.1948). A poet, lyricist, story writer and critic, Manorama has published poetry collections including *Kishalaya, Bratati, Jahnaratira Muhna, Ekla Naiira Git* and *Chitra Au Chitra.* She is also a winner of the state Sahitya Akademi award.

Soubhagyabant Maharana (b.1951). Beginning with *Shagua Kshatar Sahar* until *Prati Ishwar,* Soubhagya has a published over sixteen collections in Odia. He is the recipient of Odisha Sahitya Akademi award. Two of his significant works include *Maya Darpan* and *Aparampara.* A retired insurance officer, he also writes essays and critical articles on contemporary literature.

Bhagaban Jayasingh (b.1952). An eminent poet and critic, Bhagaban has published six volumes of poetry in Odia, besides a volume of poetry in English translation. Recently his poetry book *The Dapples of Darkness* has been published by Black Eagle Books (Ohio, USA). His critical book *Door to Despair: Modernism in Odia Poetry* was published in 2012. He has since retired as Principal of a government postgraduate college on the seaside city of Puri.

Aparna Mohanty (b.1952). A well-known woman poet, Aparna has retired from Kendrapara Autonomous College as Head of the Department of Odia. Her publications include *Abyakta Atmiyata, Asati, Atithi, Jhia Pain Jharkatia* and *Tirthayatra*. One can locate her poetry at the intersection of feminism and poetry. Her poetry mostly ranges from the celebration of gender, female sexuality to motherhood.

Aswini Kumar Mishra (b.1953). A retired civil administrator, Aswini has published over fifteen books of poetry. His poetry has appeared in national and international journals, including Kavya Bharati, Indian Literature and Wasifiri. He had earlier served as Secretary Odisha Sahitya Akademi. Some of his most admired collections are *Nakha Darpan, Sakshatar Din, Mahabatyar Akshi, Sabu Maa Eka Pari* and *Matimunhas*.

Haraprasad Parichha Pattnaaik (b.1953). Haraprasad is the author of several poetry collections, the most recent of which is *Nastahoijibar Moha*. A PhD in creative writing, he has retired as Director, Odisha Textbook Bureau. Some of his well-admired collections of poetry are *Nirabatar Swar, Eka Eka Sanyasi, Athaya Surya* and *Aranyare Kete Din*. He has received Utkal Surya Samman and Odisha Sahitya Akademi award.

Hrushikesh Mallick (b.1955). Hrushikesh has published ten books of poetry so far, besides a book of criticism. His debut volume of poetry, *Dhan Saunta Jhia* bagged him the state Sahitya Akademi award for 1988. Later on, Hrushikesh received the prestigious Sarala award for *Jeje Dekhinathiba Bharat* in 2016. Some of his very important collections of poetry are *Ujuda Kshetar Gita, Dharmapatni, Sakshi Surya Chandra* and *Basusen.*

Pravasini Mahakud (b.1955). A state Sahitya Akademi awardee, Pravasini has published a number of poetry anthologies, beginning with *Muhurat Muhurta,* and followed by *Adharashila, Gypsie Jhia* and *Kehi Jane Subhangi.* Her poems have appeared in English and Hindi translation.

Shatrughna Pandab (b.1955). Recipient of the Odisha Sahitya Akademi award for poetry, Satrughna has also earned his reputation as a critic. He has published seven anthologies of poetry; and some of his well-known anthologies are: *Nishwasar Dalapatra* and *Mishra Dhrupad.* The latter has won him the prestigious Sarala award.

Amarendra Khatua (b.1957). A member of the Indian Foreign Service, Amarendra has recently retired as Foreign Secretary from the Ministry of External Affairs. He writes both in Odia and English. His Odia poetry collections include *Shabdar Nirapata, Samartha Biparjaya, Jiban Jatrar Nanabaya* and *Drushya Apahanch.*

Prasanna Kumar Mohanty (1959). A poet, short story writer and critic, Prasanna's poetry collections are *Nirbasanaru Shabda, Pratyayar Paridhi, Priya Sakha, Pade Pade Yudha* and *Alpa Jaha Baki.* He has received

Jhankar Award and Padma Charan Patnaik Poetry award. He has since retired from BJB Autonomous College, Bhubaneswar as its Principal.

Binapani Panda (b.1959). An MA in Economics, Binapani has been awarded by various literary organisations, including Sucharita, Kadambini and Odisha Lekhika Sansad. Her poetry collections include *Nija Nija Akash, Kichhi Katha Kichhi Nirabata, Kakar Bundare Surya, Tanutirtha* and *Dwi Parna*.

Pitambar Tarai (b.1959). Pitambar has published thirteen volumes of poetry, including one collection of poems for children. He is the recipient of Kalinga Sahitya Samman, Gokarnika Kabita Samman and Odisha Sahitya Akademi award. Some of his well-known collections include *Bunde Luhar Pithire Samudra, Abhajan* and *Chira Chaitar Chitha*.

Senapati Pradyumna Keshari (b.1959). Pradyumna has published eight collections of poetry including *Mahu Muhan, Adya*, besides *Putana*, which has gone into several reprints ever since its appearance, a decade ago. He has been honored by Prajatantra Prachar Samiti with its Bishub award. He is also a recipient of Gangadhar Meher Kabita Samman.

Pradeep Biswal (b.1960) has published five volumes of Odia poetry, besides a few collections in translation. His poetry collections *Bhumishparsha, Shesh Loka* and *Pheriba Batare* have received a fair amount of appreciation. His Facebook poems have been collected under the title *A House Within*. A senior member of the Indian Administrative Officer, Pradeep is currently placed as Additional Secretary in the Finance Department, Government of Odisha.

Surya Mishra (b.1960). A poet of substantial renown, Surya has been writing for over three decades. He has published six collections of poetry including *Satabarnar Sakal, Eka eka Sahabas* and *Likhit Nirabata*. He is currently working as a senior Information Officer under Government of Odisha.

Kamal Kumar Mohanty (b.1960). Editor of *Pahach*, an Odia literary quarterly, Kamal has published ten volumes of poetry including *Shabda Jesane Mayamruga* and *Saharare Jahna Nahin*. Presently he is working as Deputy Secretary to Government of Odisha.

Ajay Pradhan (b.1962). Ajay has published a number of poetry books, including *Bhumiparva, Shabda Satat, Anand Bhairabi*, besides some poetry reviews and articles. His poetry has been translated into English and some Indian regional languages. Presently he is working under Panchayati Raj as a village level facilitator.

Satya Pattanaik (b.1962). An Information Technology professional, Satya is based in Dublin, Ohio, USA. He has published two collections of Odia poetry, *Pashanar Prema Sangita* and *Jharka Khola Thau* and two translation collections of world literature in Odia. He edits the literary journal, *Pratishruti* from USA.

Rakshak Nayak (b.1963). A winner of Sahitya Akademi award for poetry, Rakshak has published eight volumes of poetry, besides a book of translation in Hindi. *Urdha Udan, Brahmasila, Au Sabu Sakshatare* and *Sheshahin Santaran* are some of his well-received poetry collections. He is currently working at Raj Bhavan as a senior public relations officer.

Sunil Kumar Prusty (b.1963). A former editor of some well-known literary magazines *Sachitra Vijaya, Nabalipi* and *Sishir*, Sunil's poetry collections include *Chihna Chihna Nirjanata, Deha Deula, Tanulatara Kabita* and *Asaphal Kabita*. He received the state Sahitya Akademi award for *Tanulatara Kabita*.

Sucheta Mishra (b.1965). Sucheta has published eight volumes of poetry, besides one collection of short stories, two novels and a non-fiction. Some of her notable poetry collections are *Purbarag, Uttarapaksha, Pratighat* and *Ajanma*. *Ajanma* has won her the state Sahitya Akademi award. Presently she is teaching at a local English medium school at Puri.

Amiya Ranjan Mohapatra (b.1966). Amiya has published six collections of poetry. His last collection of poems *Ahalya* is based on the mythological character Ahalya.

Suresh Nayak (b.1968). Suresh has published four collections of poetry *Bibhakta Suryoday, Nija saha Kichhi Kal, Anucharita* and *Chhayasukh*. He edits a quarterly literary magazine Akaksha from Pudicherry where he lives.

K. Shyamababu Dora (b.1969). He has published four collections of poetry including *Atmabhog* and *Shabdabhram*. He lives at Berhampur, a city in southern Odisha.

Swapna Mishra (b.1971). Swapna has published nine books of poetry, besides four novels, four collections of short stories and two books of translation. His poetry books include *Chadha Uttara, Pratham Pruthibi, Rati Pahiba Agaru* and *Udanar Duiti Dena*. She has been awarded by Odisha Lekhika Sansad, Rajadhani Pustak Mela.

Sharmistha Sahoo (b.1971) One of the most promising young poets, Sharmistha has produced three collections of poetry, including *Pabanar Pacheri* and *Jhadapakshir Gita*. A homemaker, she lives at Talcher.

Kedar Mishra (b.1972) was born in Sonepur and writes poetry in Odia. He is also known as an editor, translator, journalist, scholar, art critic, human rights worker and cultural activist. He has published five poetry collections including Sunya Abhisar and Raag Kedar and a couple of prose collections.

Manoj Kumar Meher (b.1973). Manoj has four books of poems to his credit including *Pakshi* and *Khola Jharka*. He is the recipient of Utkal Sahitya Samman for poetry. Currently he is associated with The Samaj, a leading daily newspaper of Odisha.

Bijayalaxmi Parida (b.1975). A social worker, Bijayalaxmi has authored four books of poetry. *Ei Thikanare Ghar Nahin* is her latest anthology of poems. Her earlier work *Sanja Hele Barsha* had elicited favorable response from the readers and critics alike.

Gayatribala Panda (b.1977). A well-known woman poet, novelist, journalist and editor, Gayatribala has ten collections of poetry to her credit, two of which have been translated into Hindi and English. She is the recipient of Central Sahitya Akademi "Yuba Puraskar" for poetry. She was a "writer-in-residence" at Rashtrapati Bhavan in 2015.

www.ingramcontent.com/pod-product-compliance
Lightning Source LLC
Chambersburg PA
CBHW020413080526
44584CB00014B/1307